Successful Negotiation Training Course

Essential Skills and Strategies to Negotiate Like a Pro

Mark Davies

UP

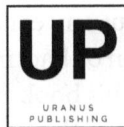

URANUS
PUBLISHING

Uranus Publishing

Disclaimer Notice:

Please note the information contained within this document is for educational and entertainment purposes only. All effort has been executed to present accurate, up-to-date, reliable, complete information. No warranties of any kind are declared or implied. Readers acknowledge that the author is not engaged in rendering legal, financial, medical or professional advice. The content within this book has been derived from various sources. Please consult a licensed professional before attempting any techniques outlined in this book.

By reading this document, the reader agrees that under no circumstances is the author responsible for any losses, direct or indirect, that are incurred due to the
use of the information contained within this document, including, but not limited to, errors, omissions, or inaccuracies.

The trademarks used are without any consent, and the publication of the trademark is without permission or backing by the trademark owner. All trademarks and brands within this book are for clarifying purposes only and are owned by the owners themselves, not affiliated with this document.

Contents

INTRODUCTION

Negotiation can be traced back to several hundreds of years ago. People often bargained products for money, clothes for certain services or lands for peace. Nowadays, this concept has been reinvented and even changed its name. We call this habit today "to negotiate." Negotiation is a brand-new notion, and it has become an art. Not anyone can do this.

Negotiation is more of a talent, an innate grace, but also a skill acquired through experience and intensive learning. Therefore, negotiation is a focused and interactive form of communication in which two or more parties in disagreement aim to reach an agreement. This will eventually solve a common problem or achieve a common goal. Negotiation enables the creation, maintenance or development of interpersonal and social relationships, in general, as business relationships or diplomatic work, in particular. It means that you know how to orient, influence, and manipulate his behavior to make him say "YES."

Reasonable people understand that they cannot unilaterally impose their will and seek common solutions, negotiated ones. Either you find yourself in war or in your own kitchen, in business or on the street, in a divorce or a conflict with terrorists, you will have to approach this method. In fact, any form of human interaction has to play a certain degree of strategy and tactics. Although there is no network or doctrines guarantee success in an infinite number of conflict situations, strategic thinking and tactical action multiply the chances of success most of the time. The strategy is a policy that may prove effectiveness in a given situation but may prove completely inapplicable to many others. It is subordinate to the overall and final objectives. A strategic line aims at long-term effects and can be materialized by deliberate or spontaneous tactical actions.

The success of negotiations varies from case to case, depending on the participants' objectives and approaches. To eliminate the risk of concluding negotiations with decisions that won't fully reflect the initial purpose, it is necessary to set from the beginning the expectations and strategy that we use. Thus, if our goal is rather to obtain a result completely according to our own interests, but under no circumstances favorable to our partner, we must be prepared to resort to persuasion and assume the risk of not getting the maximum benefits from the beginning. If we start from the idea that we can reach a compromise, the chances that the discussion to end with benefits for both sides are significantly higher. This does not mean we should give up our goal or worry that our negotiating partner might get what he wants.

However, regardless of the intended purpose or the strategy chosen, the examples presented in this book are a good starting point for training or participation in effective negotiation meetings. Why do we need this in our lives? Well, the answer is really easy. Everyone wants to make the most out of an offer, and everyone needs to feel that he has had the best fair or business so far. So, negotiation helps us improve our communication skills, ability to manipulate others' actions and take advantage of others' weaknesses. Plus, it helps us avoid conflicts and sets a common ground with other people. When you start negotiating, keep in mind that there are many ways to do this, many styles that suit different personalities. Some are more efficient with a certain kind of people, while others might fail. This is why you should read this book in order to learn how to master this art.

Communication is the foundation of negotiation. If one does not know how to talk publicly or he wrongly transmits a message, the meeting might fail from the very beginning. Then, you'll find out that negotiation has many purposes and natures, and you'll learn how to easily and effectively differentiate them. Hand in hand with these are the models of doing it that fits on different types of people

After all, our goal in life is to learn something new every day to expand our limits. Think of the chapter below as certain keys that will set you free from ignorance and limitation.

Chapter One

THE HISTORY OF NEGOTIATION

The origins

W here, how, when, and why did negotiation become a part of civilized society? It really started as barter—the direct exchange of goods or services with no money or other intermediary item of value involved.

The first swap in human history is unknown, but we know that bartering has been around for much longer than buying and selling. It grew up as a system of give-and-take that accommodated anyone who chose to participate. People found ways to fulfill their needs, whether to acquire a chunk of lamb in exchange for some pottery or to obtain jewelry for a hand-painted headpiece.

Bartering was a way to acquire life's necessities, but it was more than that—it broke down the communication barriers. When people met for the first time, bartering was a way to determine who was trustworthy and genuine, and only after mutual willingness to trade was expressed would a dialogue between the two parties ensue. (This is equally true today, particularly when so much of our interaction occurs in cyberspace.)

Bartering slowly evolved into a primitive financial arrangement in which cows, sheep, and other livestock were used as forms of currency. Plants, produce, and other agricultural items also served as currency, only to be overtaken by precious metals, stones, and finally, paper bills.

When money appeared on the scene

Cowries—marine snails boasting thick, glossy shells peppered with tiny flecks—were used in China in 1200 B.C.E. as the first money. They were widely used and even became popular in faraway places such as Africa, where some cultures continue to exchange them today. Cowries are the longest-used currency in history. In this modern era of real-time foreign exchange quotes, we still have no idea how many cowries there are to a dollar. However, as should be obvious from a swift scan of the financial news, today's economy is powered by money, and money is by far the most important element of exchange. While most of today's money is electronic—that is, it exists as a bank or some other kind of electronic balance rather than physical (paper bills and coins)—it still serves the same purpose: to facilitate exchange.

From bartering to negotiation

As primitive as this sounds, most likely, you've seen it in person. The way people bargain with each other varies from culture to culture, but you've no doubt seen bargaining take place at a yard sale or flea market. The vendor gives you a price, you give the vendor a price, and eventually, either a happy medium is decided upon, or you walk away. More often than not, the vendor inches down on her price while you inch up on your price until you're both at a number that doesn't allow either one of you to budge any further.

A different type of bargaining can be seen at an auction, where a roomful of people view the items up for sale and make their bids on the items they wish to buy. Someone makes a bid on an item. Another person makes a higher bid. Another jumps in to make a higher bid yet. This bidding continues back and forth until one person has outbid all interested parties. Today, millions of people search for, post, trade, barter, bid, and buy anything from toys they had as children to signed sports paraphernalia on eBay and other Internet auction sites. If only our sheep-trading ancestors could see us now!

Bargaining is about price

If all we did was barter, we probably wouldn't need a whole book to discuss the nature of negotiating.

Whether three baskets of corn was worth one or two chickens is more a matter of the prevailing "market" at the time than the negotiating technique employed. So what has happened to good old-fashioned bartering that merits a fancier word—and dozens of books like this one on the topic of negotiating?

The difference between bartering, or bargaining, and negotiating boils down to complexity and process. While the terms bargaining and negotiating seem synonymous, there's a difference between the two.

Bargaining, which is today's equivalent to bartering but typically incorporates money, involves streamlining wants and needs into a single focus. Before you ever step foot into your neighbor's yard sale, you well know that all the handwritten sticker prices are not permanent. Your goal is to get the item you desire at the lowest possible price. On the other hand, your neighbor's goal is twofold—to get rid of as many items as possible and get the most amount of money possible for them. When it comes to bargaining, it's all about price. Both parties focus on trying to get the best deal for themselves. In this case, money is the focal point, and that's when the price war begins: "How much?" "A dollar." "I'll give you fifty cents." "Eighty cents." "Sixty cents." "Seventy cents." "Sixty-five cents." "Deal."

When a goal becomes concentrated, it's easy to lose sight of all the things that could be important in the discussion. In the yard sale example, price takes precedence over the usefulness of the product. The purchaser never stops to think, "If I thought it was worth only fifty cents a minute ago, why do I think it's worth more now?" Although the settled price was split equally down the middle, one person spent more than she intended to, and the other person received less money for the item than he hoped to receive. So who got the bargain? Both did, in a way—the buyer still paid less than full price while the seller got more than the buyer's original offer.

Some people are said to "drive a hard bargain," meaning there's little to no chance of swaying them away from believing their offer is fair. You can't bargain with them—they are convinced that they know best or that there's someone out there who'll pay the full price. Thus, the department-store mentality is born, and the only way you're ever paying a lower price is if there's a sale.

Negotiating is about the "whole" deal

On the other hand, negotiation is about getting an agreement or settling a question between two parties. It's not always about price, and even when the price is involved, the negotiation usually isn't limited to price. Negotiating takes in all attributes of a deal. Delivery, timing, extras, the right to negotiate a future deal, a relationship all are likely to be included—and in many cases, there's no financial transaction involved at all.

Chapter Two

THE BASICS OF NEGOTIATION

Perhaps you haven't realized it, but you've been playing the negotiating game all your life. You were doing it as a child, then as an adolescent. You negotiated with your parents over free time, homework time, and dinnertime. You negotiated with your friends over swapping lunches at school or who got to pitch and who got to bat in your street baseball games. You kept it up as an adult. These days, you negotiate "business-to-consumer" to buy a car, mobile phone, or vacation package. You negotiate "consumer-to-consumer" to buy or sell stuff on Craigslist or eBay. And at work, you conduct "business-to-business" negotiations.

All through this, consciously or subconsciously, you've been developing core negotiating skills and experiences.

While those days of negotiating for baseball cards or dollhouse furniture may have long faded into history, the practice and promise of negotiating has most likely stayed with you. And it has probably become more important than ever in the life you lead today. This chapter is designed to connect your innate negotiating skills with a few basics on how today's negotiating game is played. The idea is to put some structure around what you already do. Subsequent chapters will help you build upon that basic structure so that you can round out your negotiating skillset.

The negotiation game

Strategies and Tactics

Negotiation is about getting something important that you want or need. It is about achieving a goal through a give-and-take discussion with two or more parties. It can easily be seen as a "game" (with the desired outcome and a series of strategies and tactics) and "moves" (deployed consecutively to get to that outcome).

Negotiation has a beginning, a middle, and a finish, with a strategy and desired outcome envisioned beforehand. Parties can and do make day-of-the-game course corrections, adjustments, and other changes to accommodate the moves of the counterparty as they occur. In contrast to bargaining, the outcome in a negotiation is usually multidimensional—as are the strategies and tactics you deploy to get there.

Like a game of chess, there are many possible intermediate positions you can reach to get to the ultimate goal in a negotiation. However, because there are multidimensional goals and negotiating points, in many ways, a business negotiation is more complex and involved than a game of chess. As well, there are far more interpersonal and human aspects to most negotiations.

Not a Chess Player? Nothing to Fear!

You'll do well to think of negotiating as a game, like a chess game, as you approach it. But again, unlike and beyond chess, it is often not about how well you calculate that determines the outcome, but how well you communicate and work with your counterparty. It's about how you satisfy your counterparty's needs while also taking care of your own. Unlike chess, it is often possible and always desirable to get the counterparty on your side, to work effectively and amicably with your counterparty. In a negotiation, those of you with good interpersonal skills will almost always outplay the calculating chess player!

Negotiation styles

Most negotiations will result in one of two outcomes: "win-win" or "win-lose." Understanding the various forms of negotiations allows you to identify the most relevant abilities for your profession and try to improve them. The most prevalent types of negotiations are distributive and integrative.

Distributive negotiations

Both parties aim to obtain control of a limited quantity of resources in distributive talks, also known as "distributive bargaining." This is referred to as a "win-lose" negotiation. The gain of one side equals the loss of the other. For example, a client may believe that if Company XYZ does not reduce the price of a service, they will be overcharged. The corporation may believe that lowering its price will result in a loss of money.

Integrative negotiations

An integrative negotiation, sometimes known as a "win-win," occurs when everyone benefits from the agreement. There is frequently more than one problem to be resolved; thus, tradeoffs are possible. To reach an agreement, each party receives something of value. For example, a client believes that Company XYZ should cut the cost of its service to $700, but the company argues that the pricing should remain at $900. Both parties may agree to an $800 service. Both "win" $100 in this example.

Negotiation skills for success

1. Determine and cultivate your BATNA. Your ability and desire to walk away and choose another agreement is your biggest source of power in both integrative and combative negotiations. Before arriving at the negotiation table, wise negotiators spend significant time defining and improving their best alternative to a negotiated agreement, or BATNA.

2. Approach the process with tact. Don't assume you're both on the same page about when to meet, who should be present, what your objective will be, and so on. Instead, thoroughly plan how you will negotiate ahead of time. Such procedural difficulties will pave the way for much more focused discussions.

3. Establish a rapport. Although it is not always possible to engage in small talk at the start of a negotiation (especially if you are on a tight deadline), research suggests that doing so can bring substantial benefits. If you and your counterpart spend simply a few minutes getting to know each other, you may be more collaborative and likely to achieve an agreement. Even a brief introduction phone call may make a difference if you're negotiating via email. This is one of the most important bargaining skills to learn.

4. Listen actively. When you start talking about substance, fight the temptation to worry about what you're going to say next while your counterpart is speaking. Instead, pay close attention to her ideas and then rephrase what you feel she said to ensure your

comprehension. Recognize any tough feelings lurking underneath the message, such as frustration. Not only are you likely to obtain useful information, but the other party may emulate your exceptional listening abilities.

5. <u>Pose pertinent questions.</u> Asking lots of questions that are likely to elicit good replies will help you gain more in integrative negotiation. Avoid "yes or no" queries and leading questions like "Don't you think that's a terrific idea?" Instead, ask impartial inquiries that elicit thorough responses, such as "Can you tell me about the difficulties you're experiencing this quarter?"

6. <u>Look for smart tradeoffs.</u> Parties in a distributive negotiation are frequently forced to make concessions and demands on a particular subject, such as pricing. You can use the presence of numerous concerns in integrative negotiation to get both sides more of what they desire. Specifically, attempt to find areas that are important to your opponent but that you value less. Then offer to make a concession on that subject in exchange for a concession from her on an issue that is very important to you.

7. <u>Recognize the anchoring bias</u>. Ample research reveals that the initial number mentioned in a negotiation, no matter how random, strongly influences the subsequent negotiation. You can prevent being the next victim of the anchoring bias

by making the first offer (or offers) and attempting to anchor discussions in the direction you want. If the other side does anchor first, keep your goals and BATNA in mind, pausing to revisit them as needed.

8. <u>Present many comparable offers at the same time (MESOs).</u> Instead of making one offer at a time, consider making many offers at once. If your counterpart rejects all of them, ask him which one he prefers and why. Then work on your own to improve the offer, or try to come up with a solution with the other person that pleases both of you. This method of making multiple alternatives at the same time reduces the likelihood of an impasse and can encourage more imaginative solutions.

9. <u>Contemplate a contingent contract</u>. Negotiators frequently become stopped because they disagree on how a particular scenario will play out over time. In such instances, consider creating a contingent contract—basically, a wager on how future events will unfold. For example, if you are skeptical of a contractor's assertion that he can complete your home renovation project in three months, propose a contingent contract that penalizes him for late completion and/or rewards him for early completion. He should have no trouble accepting such stipulations if he honestly believes his assertions.

10. <u>Make preparations for the implementation stage.</u> Another strategy to strengthen your contract's long-

term durability is to include milestones and deadlines to ensure that commitments are met. You might also agree in writing to meet at regular intervals during the contract's term to check-in and, if necessary, renegotiate. Furthermore, including a dispute-resolution language that requires the use of mediation or arbitration if a dispute occurs can be a good choice.

Common negotiation mistakes

Sometimes our negotiating mistakes are obvious: we reveal our bottom line by accident, attack the other party when patience is required, or get our statistics jumbled up. More often than not, though, our bargaining faults are unseen: we receive a perfectly decent offer but are ignorant that we could have gotten a better one if we hadn't succumbed to frequent blunders and traps. By learning about these five frequent negotiation blunders and how to prevent them, you can set yourself up for even greater results:

1. We do not thoroughly prepare for negotiations

The most common negotiation mistake made by corporate negotiators is rushing into a negotiation without being adequately prepared. If you have strong beliefs about what you want to receive out of the sale, you may believe you've prepared well, but this is far from the case. Wise negotiators recognize the need to devote adequate time to properly analyzing various parts of the discussion. Begin by considering your best alternative to a negotiated agreement, or BATNA, as defined by Roger Fisher, William Ury, and Bruce Patton in their book Getting to Yes: Negotiating Agreement Without Giving In. If you cannot achieve an agreement in your negotiation, your BATNA is the best course of action accessible to you. It's also a good idea to figure out your reservation value or walkaway point and try to figure out the other party's BATNA. All of these calculations will assist you in making more informed selections.

2. We are more concerned with competing than with collaborating

Fearful of being taken advantage of, newbie negotiators (and some expert ones) make unrealistic demands and resort to threats and other coercive measures to get their way. Focus on creating and claiming value for more effective negotiation. When you take the time to establish rapport and trust, both parties will feel more at ease expressing their underlying interests in the negotiation. This understanding will enable you to discover potential tradeoffs: if there is an issue about which you do not feel strongly, you may be ready to yield in exchange for a concession on an issue about which you feel passionately. Smart negotiators understand that finding win-win solutions will gain them more.

3. We rely on cognitive shortcuts

According to psychologists, we all rely on cognitive shortcuts during negotiations, especially when we are unprepared and short on time. For example, we tend to overestimate our chances of obtaining our way. And we pay more attention to visually appealing information (such as income in a job negotiation) than to less visually appealing information (such as the length of our commute) that may have a greater impact on our pleasure. Negotiation Genius: How to Overcome Obstacles and Achieve Brilliant Results at the Bargaining Table and Beyond, by Deepak Malhotra and Max H. Bazerman, highlights five typical negotiation blunders. We can enhance our negotiating skills and mitigate the negative impacts of these biases by thoroughly preparing and taking our time when negotiating.

4. We allow our emotions to control us

Along with cognitive flaws, negotiators are vulnerable to emotional biases, which can prevent them from performing at their best. Of course, our emotions and the emotions of our counterparts can provide us with useful information about how the negotiation is progressing. However, powerful emotions might prevent us from making sensible decisions, which can lead to negotiation blunders. Negotiators frequently fail to recognize how emotions influence discussions. Anger, for example, can cause us to make excessively risky decisions. And, according to Harvard Kennedy School researcher Jennifer Lerner, melancholy can cause us to overspend in negotiations. When conversations become heated, take a break to allow everyone to cool off. When you reassemble, discuss what happened, allowing everyone a chance to express their worries.

5. We take ethical detours

We tend to believe that only truly ruthless people engage in unethical negotiating. Indeed, research by Harvard Business School professor Francesca Gino and others reveals that most people are willing to cheat occasionally in negotiating and other areas when they have a financial incentive to do so and feel they will not be caught. We rationalize our actions by persuading ourselves that the other party will not feel the loss or by denying that we have done anything wrong. It is critical for all of us to be aware of ethical dangers in negotiation and to avoid absolving ourselves of even seemingly minor transgressions that violate our moral code.

Chapter Three

NEGOTIATION SCENARIOS

Positional and win-win negotiation

Although several forms of negotiation will be discussed in this book, the two most common are positional negotiating and win-win negotiating. Particularly in today's fast-paced and heavily interconnected world, you should embrace win-win negotiation as the more useful approach of these two types of negotiation.

Positional negotiation

Positional negotiating occurs when each side takes a position and is hesitant to yield much to the other. Each side is committed to its course of action—hopefully, but not always, for a business reason. Business reasons can mean things like budget or cost constraints, design constraints, specific customer needs that must be met, and so forth. Note that the party "digging in" has a business rationale for doing so.

But often—too often, really—one side takes, and tries to keep, a tough position for personal reasons: ego, a "win-at-all-costs" or "win-lose" mentality, sheer habit, or even sometimes just because they took and held a particular position successfully last time around. You should always avoid the temptation to take and hold a position in a positional negotiation for personal reasons—always ask yourself: "Is there a business reason why I'm doing this?"

At the same time, you should learn to recognize counterproductive positional negotiation tendencies in your counterparty. You may know about these tendencies before they walk into the room, or you may learn about them in the early moments of the negotiation. You'll have to think quickly once you determine that this style is in play. You can then either "fight fire with fire" or perhaps, more effectively, reach across the table and suggest that you both could accomplish a lot more and do so faster if both sides collaborated on a win-win.

Win now may mean losing later

You may win a few negotiations in the short term with a steadfast winner-take-all positional strategy. But you're likely to lose in the long term, as it takes more time and energy. And your opponents will be forced to negotiate to win as well—throwing a possible win-win out the window.

In positional negotiations, both sides become so focused on their own needs that they fail to comprehend those of the other party. A power struggle often ensues, and the parties never really get around to discussing their goals and objectives. In addition, the negativity and struggle can jeopardize long-term relationships and make the negotiation that much harder.

In short: don't be a "tough guy." It only makes things harder, and in today's competitive environment, your counterparties may simply walk.

Win-win negotiation

Instead of positional negotiation, which is really win-lose in the end, you can—and should—try to engage in a win-win style and strategy. Win-win means that both parties come away satisfied such that their needs, or at least most of their needs, are addressed and met. When both sides come away with items they want and need, agreements are made more easily, take less time, and preserve or even enhance the long-term relationship between parties—important in business as well as in personal situations.

When they don't want to play

Find the Reason

You want to make a deal to pave your parking lot, fix the roof on your building, or procure 5,000 custom integrated circuits to build into your product. You reach out to contact your favorite supplier, but he doesn't return your phone call right away. You wait a few days, and he doesn't return your phone call at all. You think your need and the business deal are pretty straightforward, and you think you have a pretty good relationship with these suppliers and contractors. So what's going on?

The first step is to simply find out why. Follow up with a phone call, leave a message if necessary, simply ask why they aren't prepared to negotiate with you. There may be a simple explanation.

If the reason why remains elusive, find out the "what" or "how." What can you put forth in order to make your request to negotiate more attractive? What can you put forth to make the negotiation quicker or easier? Can you throw some other business their way to make it more attractive? Can you be flexible with deadlines or project staging to allow the counterparty to work on other projects? If you can, you're likely to get a better deal. If you can't, you may stir up the stinging bees of a positional negotiation—or just as bad, continue to be ignored altogether.

Bottom line: it doesn't hurt to make or suggest a few concessions right in the beginning. You want to get the counterparty to the table, and you want to get them to the table feeling positive.

Separating the people from the problem

Suppose you're just getting started on what might be a tense negotiation with a state regulatory agency on environmental compliance concerning your business. Your dander is up. This isn't going to be good; you can feel it. And your negotiating partner is already writing off the counterparty as a "bunch of tree-huggers who don't deserve the time of day." You've met with this team before, and their body language, among other things, reflected that they might not just feel so good about you guys, either.

Is this negotiation likely to get off on the right foot? Are you going to be able to stick to the facts and issues? Will you be able to stay on task? Are you likely to be successful at hammering out a win-win solution quickly while also building a long-term trusting relationship?

Probably not, unless you can separate the people from the problem and deal with each in its own sphere.

One of the core principles pervasive to the practice of effective negotiation is the idea of separating the people—the personal emotions, perceptions, and biases inherent in a negotiation (because people do negotiations!)—from the real issues being discussed.

Here are a few techniques for dealing with the people issues and keeping them from sundering your win-win problem-solving efforts:

1. Put your (negative) perceptions in check. Sure, the environmental agency negotiators don't "live in the real world" of running a business. But don't assume that they aren't aware of what that real world is all about. If your negative perceptions turn out to be right—that they are insensitive about the needs of your business—take a short time-out to give them an objective and factual overview of what you do and how the environmental regulations make that painful.

2. Realize that they probably want the same thing you do. At the end of the day, they want a solution too, and they want it quickly. They don't want to have to put excessive time and energy into the case, and they probably don't want to deal with your people's issues any more than they have to! They would like to walk away with a deal and a relationship.

3. Practice empathy. The counterparty's negotiators are people, too, trying to be successful in achieving their goals without too much pain and suffering. They have families to support and other work to do, just like you do. They have a job to get done. Respect that and help them do it, and they'll do the same.

4. Take time-outs. When basketball coaches sense things are becoming too emotional and personal, they call a time-out to take players' minds off the game at hand. You can—and should—do this, too. If you sense tension or interpersonal conflict, don't let it overheat. Instead, take a break so that everyone can cool off. Better yet, use the break time to discuss common ground topics like your recent vacations or the new city recreation center. Whatever the topic, the goal is to establish rapport and reinforce the fact that you're both "human."

5. Keep communications effective. Listen actively, and talk when it's your turn. Don't use harsh or bullying language, and don't react or respond to theirs. While you might put them on the defensive insofar as your problem is concerned, don't put them on the defensive personally. Never talk down to anyone, and if they talk down to you, just ignore it.

It comes down to this: Always think positive and realize that the proverbial glass is half full when it comes to working with people. When you can do that successfully, you'll put the personal conflicts aside and free up your team—both teams, really—to deal more effectively with the problem.

Again, Negotiating Is Everywhere

Put simply, everyone negotiates. Parents negotiate with teachers; husbands negotiate with wives;

brothers negotiate with sisters; defense attorneys negotiate with prosecuting attorneys; and so forth. Even children exercise a form of negotiating. It's funny how adults are still playing the game of "I'll trade you this for that," albeit in a more sophisticated and refined manner.

While you may play down these personal-life negotiations, you probably negotiate a lot if you're in any kind of business or professional environment. Deals are done, budgets are created, and money is spent or acquired through negotiation. You may be finding yourself vying for a multimillion-dollar deal for your business—or for a $150 admission ticket to a trade show you'd like to attend. Both are negotiations, and both require much of the same set of skills.

In sum, negotiating is about getting what you want. Win-win negotiating is about getting what you want through the recognition of your goals and the goals of a counterparty and finding a peaceful solution that sends everyone away with maximum satisfaction with the minimal time consumed. In today's rapidly moving world, time is of the essence. Luckily, the real-time information available at our fingertips helps us find that win-win more quickly and precisely than ever before.

Chapter Four

INTEGRATIVE NEGOTIATIONS

Distributive Vs. integrative negotiation

If you assume the pie is fixed in negotiation science, you must participate in distributive negotiation to negotiate for a share of the pie. On the other hand, if you assume the pie can grow with cooperation, you will participate in integrative negotiation. This is also called interest-based bargaining or a win-win situation. So, is the pie always fixed, or can it be expanded? There are many situations when the pie is fixed, and cooperating to find a middle ground through compromise is the best solution. Other times, one or both parties could come up with creative ways to increase the pie so that neither must compromise and instead can collaborate.

These win-win situations are ideal but can often take time to develop, negotiate, and execute. Again, finding these creative solutions is an interest-based bargain and implies talking about and learning the interests of both parties. Remember leading with interests rather than an outcome will help you close the deal.

How to move from distributive to integrative

Moving from a distributive to an integrative negotiation requires you to be creative and find value. The following are the three steps required to move the conversation from distributive to an integrative negotiation:

1. Build Trust

2. Ask the right questions

3. Make equivalent simultaneous offers

<u>Build trust</u>

Trust is essential in a negotiation because it prevents emotions from taking over and a positional negotiation dominating. It also allows for a more open exchange of interests, allowing the negotiations to reach more of the middle region of ZONA if the pie is fixed or reach new creative solutions if the pie can be expanded. However, with regards to business negotiation, reliability is the most important to the foundation of building trust. It behooves you to prove you are reliable leading up to the negotiation by sending any required documents on time, showing up on time, not rescheduling negotiations, and coming ready to negotiate.

The old tactics of delaying the negotiation, walking out, and seeming unavailable only fuel positional negotiating and will likely end a deal. Think of a time when you agreed on a deal, but the other party took too long to make the offer official. For some, it almost tempted them to re-negotiate; for others, it often does. After establishing reliability, it is essential to establish trust. It may seem counterintuitive, but to show trustworthiness, you must focus on the needs and interests of the other person instead of your needs.

In Game theory, the most successful outcome is when one partner matches exactly what the other partner chooses only if they know what the other wants. We discuss some aspects of how body language plays a role in building trust in the last section, and we've also previously covered Dale Carnegie's principles to get someone to like you and trust in you in the Concise.

Ask the right questions

Distributive negotiation, as we learned, refers to a fixed pie, while integrative negotiation refers to an expanded pie where everybody wins. Some negotiations are inherently distributive, like when haggling over price with a street vendor. That is because the price is the only issue on the table. However, many issues can be uncovered, thereby expanding the fixed pie.

Asking the right questions is vital to understand the other person's interests and uncover their BATNA. Only then can you find creative terms to the negotiation that would find agreement with both parties. The goal of asking questions is to move from a debate to a discussion. Imagine finding an expert in a subject matter and trying to negotiate profit sharing for a nationwide seminar series.

On the other hand, since you are providing the capital, marketing, and promotion, you should have a larger share of the profits. Arguing on those terms will never move the negotiation forward. Instead, if the expert asked you what he can do to de-risk your investment, and you asked the expert what he would need to do to appeal to a larger audience and what he needs to meet his expectations, then the terms of the negotiation just expanded considerably. The type of questions one should be asking is circular or open-ended. They don't have a predetermined response. Instead, they aim to uncover the basis of each other's position as well as any potential terms on which to negotiate on. Asking the expert what dollar value he would put on his expertise is a leading question, one that from the start implies you think his or her dollar value will never command a higher share of the profits.

Leading questions will only make the expert take a defensive stance, bringing you back to a debate instead of a discussion. Do not ask leading questions in a negotiation.

The Story of the Local Baker: There once was a local baker whose experience in negotiation was a lesson for many students of the art. The business was declining for the baker, and he even thought of closing his bakery at the end of the year until a young prince smelled the delicious aroma of freshly baked dough. The prince wanted to hire the baker to bake goods for this weekend's party at the royal palace. The prince wanted to impress the king by bargaining for a good deal. The prince asked for a price that was just above cost and significantly below what the baker would typically sell his goods for. The baker realizing that his BATNA was to close his bakery within a year, decided to see how else he could make the terms more favorable.

He asked the prince, "What type of event is this? Do you hold events often where you would need baked goods?" The prince told him that this weekend's event was to celebrate spring and that he always holds weekly events to celebrate people and nature. The Baker then told him that the price the prince is asking for would leave very little profit for him, but if he were to allow the Baker to sell additional special treats at the party like chocolate at the typical retail price, then he would be happy to bake goods every weekend for the young prince. The prince elated that he got a bargain, happily accepted. The Baker, having secured a new source of consistent income, happily rejoiced.

The moral of this story is to ask questions to uncover terms that make a negotiation favorable for both parties.

Multiple Equivalent Simultaneous Offers (MESOs)

This strategy is to focus your attention on the middle offer. Think Goldilocks and the three bears. She didn't like the extremes of temperature in the porridge or the hardness of the bed. Instead, she preferred the middle choice. It is helpful to uncover terms and move to an integrative negotiation, but it is an especially effective strategy when negotiating with a team because of their different preferences, interest, and needs.

Imagine you offer another party the choice between a fast and expensive car or a slow and affordable car. If they lean more towards the slow and affordable car, you automatically uncover the preference for an affordable car over a fast one and can then give them a third option of an even slower but very affordable car. MESOs help uncover preferences or additional terms to negotiate on without using open-ended questions or in addition to a constructive discussion.

Alternatively, MESOs can be used to demonstrate flexibility and willingness to be agreeable with multiple options making the other party feel that they have a choice when all choices work equally well for you. MESOs require a lot of pre-negotiation planning but can be used in the beginning, middle, or end of negotiation to uncover preference, reset the anchor, and continue to move towards terms that are agreeable to both parties. The important planning aspect of this negotiation technique is setting up a scoring system for all the different issues or terms. If the other party's preferences overlap between offers, you can quickly calculate whether the cherry-picked offer is still acceptable for you.

The obvious use case for this type of negotiation is when there are many issues, many terms, or many parties to negotiate. If this use case applies to you, then be sure to write out all the possible combinations of terms that you would accept and rank them according to which is most profitable for you and which is likely most profitable for the person or team you are negotiating with. Unlike in single offers where you lead with your interest, you don't divulge all your interests except for a few in this scenario. You will find that while the other party thinks you are making a concession, you agree to your 4th or 5th interest.

More complex negotiations
Building contingency

Sometimes a deal involves risks. Adding contingencies to the terms of a deal can help enforce the terms, manage future disagreements, and reduce chances for litigation. You may have noticed that real estate owners of apartment rentals are beginning to de-risk against future disasters by requiring tenants to purchase renter's insurance for damage to their property, liability insurance for damage to their person, and sometimes even crime insurance theft of tenant's property. Homeowners now build a contingency bonus payment if the contractors were to finish their work before the deadline and a penalty if the work exceeded the deadline.

If a contractor refuses to sign with that contingency in this situation, then ask them why, and the answer might be that there is a chance the project will become overdue. In this case, armed with new information, it is time to renegotiate the final price to reflect the increased uncertainty of the delivery date. Complex negotiations involve risk, and understanding the risks helps you come to a more aggregable final offer. In the case of buyer and contractor, the contractor has all the risk information, leading to an asymmetry of information. That is why contingencies matter.

Additionally, contingencies help to solve contract breaches without the need for additional negotiations. If a contingency is placed to address each potential breach, the law becomes black and white by signing a contract, avoiding legal fees. Although an annoying practice for renters, using the same landlord-tenant lease example, while the lease is filled with multiple ways to breach the contract and multiple different penalties associated with breaching the contract, it also adds a term to the contract that if there are any legal fees due, they would be automatically owed by the tenant in the event that it is due to an issue that the landlord was not able to think of and list at the time of the contract. The lease example is a little unfair because the tenant typically has little buying power to negotiate the terms--that's why we rely on the government to protect our fair housing rights in markets where the seller has no incentive to negotiate.

There is a valuable lesson from carefully reading a lease agreement. It will show you how much landlords have de-risked their investment and future liability by using contingencies in contracts. In other situations where both parties have more to gain, contingencies help reduce risk, increase incentives to complete the deal, and allow the contract to solve instances of disagreement or breach of contract.

The contingencies in this case help get a deal closed by assuring both parties of payment or nonpayment in the event of a risk occurrence.

Perspective-taking

The adage of withholding judgment until you've walked a mile in someone else's shoes is also true during negotiations. Don't be offended by an extreme first offer, assuming you didn't have the chance to make it yourself and anchor the negotiation terms. We learned to always try to uncover additional terms and preferences through asking questions or by using MESOs. One more tool to uncover interests and motivations is perspective-taking. Imagine a famous chef suddenly wants to sell their restaurant at the highest bid offer. It is time to try and understand why.

Are they nearing retirement? Do they have teenagers going to college, and they need to pay their tuition? Maybe your company has secured bargain deals for retirement vacations, or your company offers a college scholarship specifically to children of culinary experts. You could add these additional terms to the deal to obtain a more attractive offer for both parties. Using perspective taking will allow you to uncover even more potential negotiation points, especially when each party's ZONA never overlaps based on existing terms such as a low bid and a high reservation price. Maybe the retirement home requires a fixed deposit that can only be reached with a high bid, but by offering a retirement home discount that your company already has negotiated for its own employees, then you can settle on a more reasonable price point.

Rebuilding trust

In a situation where trust was lost because of an argument, an accidental insensitivity, or any reason, the most important building block to bring the other party back to the negotiation table is building trust again. This begins by using Dale Carnegie's lessons of getting people to like you by learning everything you can about them and their business and then shifting the conversation to what they want and need. Hold your demands until the end of the negotiation. After you have barely rekindled the trust by showing gratitude for the past relationship and concern for their concerns, the next step is to make a unilateral concession in the industry. This has been shown many times to regain trust. However, the order of events is important. If the unilateral concession was made without first meeting with the other party and listening to their concerns, it would appear as just a cheap move to close a deal. After the unilateral concession, you then need to explicitly state all the concessions you've made and all the considerations you are willing to make. Often, we assume people remember everything we've done for them, but they don't. Reminding them of all the concessions you made reminds them of your effort in this negotiation. Because of Adam's Equity Theory that we learned in the Leadership Principles Concise Read, we know that if the concessions are unequal, that the other party will expect that it is their turn to make a concession. This is when you finally explicitly state your demands and explain your demand and what they are motivated by. Now the negotiation should be back to before the point it fell apart.

Value claiming in negotiation

We negotiate if we are attempting to achieve a goal and require another party with different preferences. Most discussions have two objectives: value claiming and value creation. Value can be described as anything you want to achieve out of a negotiation, such as more money, a consulting contract, a new rug, the resolution of a quarrel, and so on.

Value claiming, also known as distributive negotiation or single-issue negotiation, entails attempting to take as much of the pre-existing value off the table for yourself—and away from the opposing side. Negotiating the purchase of a rug at a foreign bazaar is one example. Value creation, also known as integrative negotiation, is looking for other sources of value that may be brought to the table to expand the pie beyond the most obvious issue, such as pricing. When negotiating a job, for example, you might go beyond money to cover problems like vacation time, responsibilities, flex time, and so on to create value for both sides.

At times, a negotiation will only have a distributive component—that is, there will only be possibilities to claim value rather than produce value. When bargaining for that rug, for example, you might have a hard time coming up with other points to bring up. Far more frequently, though, hidden sources of value can be added to the discussion to produce value.

Professional negotiators must become adept in distributive and integrative negotiation to prevail at the bargaining table. Ideally, you should be able to produce more value by negotiating cross-issue trades and then claim the lion's share of that value for yourself via distributive negotiation tactics.

<u>Prepare yourself for value claiming</u>

Professor Leigh L. Thompson (Northwestern University) in his book "The Mind and Heart of the Negotiator: Bargaining for Value", defines four critical actions you can take to strengthen your negotiating skills and completely prepare to claim value.

<u>Evaluate and improve your BATNA</u>. In a negotiation, your best alternative to a negotiated agreement, or BATNA, is frequently your most powerful source of leverage. When you have a viable alternative, you will be able to walk away from any agreement that falls short of your BATNA. Wise negotiators not only examine their BATNA prior to bargaining but also spend significant time attempting to enhance it. For example, a job seeker may continue to look for other opportunities while negotiating a specific offer, or they may attempt to negotiate one or more offers simultaneously.

Calculate, but do not reveal, your reserve point. In a negotiation, your reserve point is usually a figure or offer that symbolizes what you need to get at the table in order to pursue your BATNA. For example, if you had a job offer from Firm A for $70,000 per year and want to do better in discussions with Firm B, you would determine the lowest amount (such as $75,000 or $80,000) Firm B might pay you to persuade you to accept the position. Because your reservation point, also known as your walkaway point or bottom line, is the smallest amount you are ready to accept, it is generally best not to disclose it or your BATNA with your counterpart across the table, even if you trust and like them, lest they exploit this information.

Investigate the opposing party's BATNA and reservation point. It is critical to estimate your own BATNA and reservation point and your counterpart's BATNA and reservation point. This information will assist you in determining how far you can push the opposite side. You can develop these estimates by considering and investigating the other party's choices and resources, such as how much money they may have and what other bargaining chances may occur for them.

Examine the ZOPA. You will be able to analyze the zone of probable agreement, or ZOPA, once you have a notion of each party's reservation point. According to Harvard Business School professors Deepak Malhotra and Max H. Bazerman in their book

Negotiation Genius, the ZOPA comprises the range of all conceivable bargains that both sides would find acceptable. For example, if you, as a job seeker, would take a minimum of $75,000 from a firm and your research indicates that they may pay you up to $85,000, your ZOPA is $75,000-85,000. Your ZOPA will also assist you in setting an ambitious but achievable goal, such as $85,000.

By conducting this type of analysis, you will be well placed for effective value claiming in both distributive and integrative negotiations.

Chapter Five

STYLES AND PERSONALITIES IN NEGOTIATION

I always stressed the idea of broad preparation for any negotiation, covering everything from goals, musts, and wants to the details of the product, price, and competitive landscape, all the way to knowing your counterparty and the negotiating venue. This broad view tells you what to prepare; as you approach the negotiation, you'll want to dive into the detail of these areas as time and access to information permit.

As you try to "see the outcome," you should recognize that one of the key variables is the negotiating style of the counterparty—particularly the leading spokesperson of the counterparty. The interpersonal dynamic between you and your team members—and the leader and the members of the counterparty team —can have a lot to do with the final outcome.

This chapter is about "seeing" the negotiation style you'll have to deal with (and understanding your own, don't forget) and then getting a handle on how your styles mesh and how to counteract the differences in style. Put simply, oil and water at the negotiating table will not bring the best win-win agreement.

In this chapter, I will examine the ins and outs of seven distinct negotiating styles, give some additional insight into negotiating personalities—the building blocks of negotiating styles—and then finish with a summary of how to deal with difficult styles and personalities.

Why is style important?

Negotiators are people, and people are different

As you start to internalize the basics of negotiating (why negotiate, what to negotiate for, how to give and take, and how to prepare), you should also keep in mind other essential pieces of the puzzle. One of these is people. No matter what the negotiation is about, you're negotiating with people at the end of the day. Negotiators come from all walks of life—all personalities, all experiences, and all styles. They can be professional negotiators or negotiating professionals (remember the difference?). They can be people just like you, but many times they're not like you at all!

Part of the preparation process involves understanding and recognizing the different negotiating styles, personality styles, and personas you'll find in the negotiating world. Not only will you encounter these styles, but you'll most likely adopt one or more of them yourself, depending on the situation, your objectives, and your own personality. In today's fast-negotiation world, you may have to recognize these styles very quickly and do so through relatively impersonal means, i.e., not by face-to-face communication.

Below I will identify seven common negotiating "styles" you'll often find across the negotiating table, one of which likely describes you as well! If someone is an "intimidator," can you recognize that through initial contacts? The quicker you can, the better.

The Intimidator

Keeping You Off Balance

Intimidators prey on emotions. They want you to feel as if the negotiation is personal—and if something goes wrong, it's your fault. They put you on the defensive and try to separate you from your rational self. They hope your bruised ego will prevent you from looking objectively at the negotiation as it unfolds.

Is this psychological warfare? You bet! Intimidators take advantage of your human side, focusing less on the business aspect of what you're trying to accomplish and more on the personal side. They hope you'll do anything—give anything—to seek peace and find balance in the negotiation, even if it means your side has to cede ground. They hope you never regain equilibrium that you give in to their demands just so you can be done with this phase of the deal.

Remember: a deal done under stress and duress is likely to be a bad deal.

Recognizable Characteristics

If your counterparty is shouting or pounding a fist or slapping papers down on the table, you see an intimidator in action. These people are loud, talk fast, make hurried movements, and often resort to profanity to make a point. They interrupt constantly. Again, they're trying to get you to focus on the antics, prevent you from thinking clearly, distract you, and cause you to lose your train of thought, especially when they don't like what they're hearing or are not getting their way. They want you to jump from rational negotiator mode to "people pleaser" mode, to jump from getting what you want to placate their needs. Don't go there!

Intimidators will make demands, not suggestions or requests. Rather than accepting that you're proposing a workable solution benefiting both of you, they'll tell you that they're insulted by an offer of anything less than exactly what they demanded in the first place. They may start yelling again and even throw out a few expletives for extra drama.

Intimidators push you around and try to frighten or annoy you with threats. They might threaten to call off the entire negotiation, bring in someone from upper management, or withdraw their business altogether. Quite often, these behaviors are bluffs; you should handle them accordingly.

Be aware that not all intimidators are loud and blustery. Some may take the quiet approach, shrewdly manipulating you with a barely recognizable yet penetrating insolence. Their ploy may even be delivered more through body language than verbal antagonism. Condescending by nature, they know how to crawl under your skin with just a look, hand gesture, or blink of an eye. They may not intimidate you with brazen scare tactics but may instead act as if they're far above you in every way.

Whatever the approach, an intimidator may just patronize your business sense. But when an intimidator also patronizes your person—look out!

Counteracting the Intimidator

The best way to defend against intimidators is to avoid stooping to their level. Stay calm, focused, and in control. When the intimidator starts raising his voice, keep yours at an even tone. Displaying no emotion whatsoever and going on about your business shows them that you won't take the bait. You're a professional, and your objective is to reach an agreement, not to get into a fight.

Dealing with the Intimidator in Presidential Politics

In late 2016, the "going about your business" tactic was clearly on display in the first presidential debate of the fall 2016 campaign. Donald Trump ranted, showed emotion, and even exhibited annoying and sometimes aggressive body language and stage positioning to his counterparty, Hillary Clinton. But she didn't flinch, and she simply went on about her business. That got under his skin, and he showed even more of that behavior, which left a negative impression on the audience and caused him to "lose" that first debate as much as anything else.

As we found out from the election results, countermanding the intimidator may not always win in the end. Nonetheless, rising above the bluster can help you out a lot along the way.

Never shout or use abusive language. That only escalates the conflict and takes you away from the issue at hand. Instead, stay calm, focused, and in control. Avoid emotional involvement and work to get the focus back on the issues at hand. Ask open-ended questions to avoid being brushed off with simple yes-

and-no answers. Your goal is to force your counterparty to talk about the issues, the real reasons you're both there. In so doing, the intimidator might cool down and realize you aren't playing his game.

If he tries to intimidate you by threatening to pull out of the negotiation altogether, try to feel out how serious this threat is. Offer a few noncritical concessions—or ask point-blank what he plans to do if he pulls out. The goal is to call his bluff. If he leaves the table as an intimidation tactic, remember that he'll probably be back if your negotiating position is solid, to begin with—and he'll be weaker as a result of the called bluff. It's a gamble on your part but one probably worth taking to neutralize the intimidation.

As most negotiations are gone sour or uncomfortable, it helps to take a time-out to regroup and cool the emotions. You'll cool your own, and you're likely to diminish the thunder of your opponent, particularly if it was a ploy in the first place. You might even ask him point-blank, over a refreshment, "Why are you so angry and difficult to talk to? We could get this done much quicker and more effectively if we simply hold ourselves as equals and have a productive conversation." As you might surmise, this tactic works in both business and personal negotiations.

The Flatterer

<u>Positive, Complimentary—and Insincere</u>

Like the intimidator, the flatterer focuses more on your emotions than on facts and logic. The difference: the flatterer gets personal by loading the negotiation with positive but insincere remarks. The idea, once again, is to get an emotional response, deflect you from the facts, and throw you off balance.

The flatterer operates under the assumption (mostly correct) that everyone loves to receive compliments, so she lays it on to boost your ego. You may hear glowingly positive comments about your business style, your product, your team, your company, or even your personal appearance. When the car salesperson tells you how good you look driving in a particular car, take the compliment with a grain of salt.

The point of this ego-stroking is to appeal to your emotional side, to give you a false sense of reality, even a false sense of security. For example, the flatterer may try to make you believe that you have the upper hand—that you're "winning" the negotiation—so why not "give us a break" and offer a few minor concessions?

Recognizable Characteristics

Since the flatterer attempts to render the negotiation more personal than professional, you might see a lot of smiles and compliments right off the bat. Throughout the negotiation, your counterparty might say something like, "I know I can't pull one over on you, Amanda, that's why I'm giving it to you straight right now." The hope is that you'll be so flattered at the recognition of your expert, seasoned negotiating skills that you'll bask in the glory, become complacent, and ultimately lose your edge in the negotiation.

Keep an Eye on the Faces

Since extreme flattery is a form of dishonesty, its presence can be a good indicator as to whether the other party plans to fulfill her side of the bargain. Try to recognize speech patterns and facial expressions when the flattering statement is made—and compare those patterns to what you see when the counterparty agrees with one of your requests.

Never underestimate the ability of body language, facial expressions, and speech to tell you what's really going on.

When the other party turns you into the main subject of the discussion, it becomes a challenge to stay focused on the details of the issues you're talking about. It's easy to get sucked into all that flattery, not to mention the pleasant, nonconfrontational language. But you must focus on your purpose for the negotiation: to achieve business (or personal) goals in a win-win approach—not to have your ego stroked.

Counteracting the Flatterer

The flatterer, like the intimidator, is an expert at tapping into your emotions. Such an approach is not only a style but a habit. Your approach should be the same as with the intimidator: Redirect the focus back to the issues at hand. Stop and redirect the conversation, even start taking notes, as it shows the counterparty you mean business. Stay calm, ignore the flattery, and don't let it frustrate you. Redirect by asking open-ended questions that force your counterparty to talk about the details of the negotiation.

Another defensive tactic is to change your tone of voice to one of total indifference. Don't use inflections or interject any personality into your speech. If you project a steely, emotionless image to the other party and refuse to react to the sweet talk, she will eventually realize that you're not succumbing to her tactics.

Another tactic is to involve a third party, either one present at the negotiation or brought in for the task. Getting a manager or technical expert involved can help—it takes the focus off you and redirects the negotiation to the facts and the results. When you get flattered by a car salesperson, it's time to bring in your spouse or grown child to diffuse the flattery. In business, bringing in another party, especially a manager or other authority, will help.

Aside from letting the flattery get you off track, the worst thing you can do is return the flattery. Don't go there. If you do, she's roped you into a mutual admiration compact and opened the door for more flattery and even less serious negotiating. Don't go there.

The Seducer

Magic Through Charm?

You've most definitely experienced this one before—if not in business life, certainly in your personal life. The seducer works his magic through charm. He paints a perfect picture for you and describes everything exactly as you want to hear it. But the devil is in the details—when you start to investigate, the illusion just as magically disappears. The ideal image you had in mind, one that you might have just made a concession for, disappears as you uncover more details.

By all appearances, it's a win-win deal. Only after they ring you up at the register do you find out that the rebate comes after the fact as store credit coupons that you must use to buy something else rather than applying it toward the home theater purchase. The salesperson/negotiator made the discount a central part of the deal, only to pull the rug out from under you. You were seduced.

Recognizable Characteristics

The seducer is crafty and sometimes unethical, and he will make attractive offers and concessions to you throughout the negotiating process. Once he has you hooked, he'll reel you in by telling you what you want to hear—often in half-truths. "You'll get 10 percent off"—but it isn't a discount; it's a credit toward your next purchase. As soon as you commit, he points to the fine print, and the deal he really offers begins to emerge.

The seducer may blame "the system" behind him. You'll hear excuses like, "The paperwork is still being finalized," "My manager hasn't authorized it yet," or "I'm waiting to hear from my attorney." The deal may be sped up—or slowed down—to meet his objective. He might speed it up to get you out of the store before you notice, or he might slow it down by distracting you with some other detail, a phone call or contingency, so once again, you don't notice the change in the promise. When the counterparty seems to be deliberately speeding up or slowing down, lookout.

Counteracting the Seducer

Protecting yourself from the seducer is simple: Don't deal. Make the seducing point seem unimportant or irrelevant: "I was planning to pay cash anyway." If it's too late and the agreement has been made, revisit the negotiation and get a higher authority involved—an attorney or a manager or some such person. Even the threat to do that can neutralize the counterparty, and he may retract the seducing element(s) on his own. If you've recognized the signs early on, simply leave the negotiation and seek other alternatives.

Research can be your best friend here. The more you find out about the party you'll be dealing with in negotiations, the better your chances of identifying a seducer early and staying out of the way. For instance, if you're shopping for electronics, a review of the seller's website or a flip through their weekly ad circular can clue you into the types of deals you may hear about on the sales floor.

If you decide to continue negotiating with the seducer, be sure to be informed of every detail of the agreements made. Ask lots of questions. Know what you're getting and how you're getting it. Facts neutralize the seducer, as they do many other types of negotiators who appeal to your emotions. Take notes where appropriate. It lets the seducer know you're paying attention to every word.

Finally, be skeptical. A little healthy skepticism never hurts in any negotiation.

The Complainer

<u>Working the Guilt Angle</u>

Although the complainer is not as deceitful and unfair as other negotiating personalities covered thus far, she can still undermine the negotiation. The complainer is typically an insecure negotiator—or a master at the ploy—who really wants to be heard and understood. Once she's gotten her say, this counterparty becomes more reasonable and more pleasant to work with.

Recognizable Characteristics

Complainers succeed when they make you feel bad about what you're asking for or what you need or want out of a negotiation. They induce guilt, motivating you to moderate your requests to keep them happy.

Complainers can sometimes come across as positional negotiators, not win-win negotiators (see Chapter 2). This is because they don't appear to look past their own needs. They may appear unwilling to budge from their position, but they're really looking for you to come up with the deal that makes them not complain anymore.

You may hear statements like, "How can you expect me to give you a free warranty when you're already asking me for a discount?" or "You have no idea how expensive it is for production to make the kinds of changes you're asking for," or "I'll get fired if I offer you that deal." If you listen closely, there's a cry for help couched in those sentences.

When complainers begin statements with "How can you" and "You have no idea," they want you to back down a little and help them out. They can take a perceived weakness—if the ploy works—and turn it into a strength, thereby giving up less than they otherwise might have.

Counteracting the Complainer

You'll need a good ear and an empathetic heart to guard against the complainer. If you handle the situation with the right amount of patience and understanding, you'll get through the fluff and the apparent dug-in position. You can then help her realize that a win-win may well be in sight, which can, in turn, allay the fears and complaints. She wants your understanding, and perhaps you can give her some without giving away the store.

Don't Just Listen—Listen Actively!

No matter the negotiation, and no matter the style of the negotiators, your job doesn't end at simply being there, hearing, or even passively listening. You must listen actively. Paraphrase a few of the counterparty's key points to show empathy and a correct understanding of their situation. If you're conducting the conversation by email, repeat portions of the email when you reply to show you've read and understood the entire message.

Active listening is particularly effective with the complainer, but it works well in all walks of negotiating life. If you listen actively to them, they'll be more likely to listen actively to you, and you'll find that win-win much more easily.

As soon as complainers start voicing concerns, hear them out. Hear every word they say, and encourage them to say more. Nod, make eye contact and use hand gestures to let them know you're really listening. Listen actively, saying, "I see" or "That's understandable" as verbal acknowledgment. Once it's all let out, the burden is lifted, and the counterparty will relax. Most likely, she'll play well into your needs to get her complaints and negatives resolved.

Once you've finished listening to the complainer's viewpoint, ask more questions to slowly get back to the negotiation details. You might even offer a concession, a small one you saved for later, or one that you can afford to be flexible with. Show complainers that you see their point and will make an effort to make the negotiation successful for both them and you—a win-win.

The Arguer

<u>For the Love of Conflict</u>

Undoubtedly, you have certainly experienced this negotiator style in your personal life, if not your business life. The arguer is a counterparty who seems to love the conflict, thriving on disagreement—and where there isn't a conflict or disagreement, he creates one just because that's where his comfort zone lies! What you'll see is a constant argument with the main points of a discussion—and/or, more subtly, a steady and unrelenting nitpick of the smaller ones. Some arguers may start out calm and accommodating and then switch to an argumentative mode midstream in the negotiation.

Recognizable Characteristics

The arguer can be easily spotted by his steady and unprompted debates of your issues and requests. True, a negotiation can be a back-and-forth debate to get to an alternative everyone can agree on. But it turns into an argument when it gets loud and/or nitpicky and when one side or the other presses for the win. Arguers debate and nitpick more than necessary; it will seem as if they have trouble separating what's important from what isn't. They lay a lot of objections on unimportant stuff at your feet.

Counteracting the Arguer

The arguer may pounce on your every move toward progress, hoping to stall the negotiation, buy more time for his case, or prove his ability to win something. Use the plan created before the meeting to remind him that you're on a schedule and would like to stick to it to cover everything. Ignore aimless arguments by reacting to only the important ones.

When arguments dominate, ask the counterparty to explain the main concern of the argument. Focus on resolving that issue first, but be aware of meaningless arguments that might pop up along the way. Some arguers argue as a means of distraction, hoping you'll inadvertently give something away; others behave this way out of a need to score as many victories as possible, large or small. Just keep asking yourself: Do I want to be right, or do I want to win? Often you can do both. But in many situations, being right at the expense of winning ultimately means winning the battle but losing the war.

As with other strong negotiation styles, stick to your facts, ignore appeals to your emotions, and call time-outs where you think it might help. If it really gets bad, advise the counterparty that "things aren't working" and that you may be forced to leave the negotiation.

Above all, avoid becoming an arguer yourself; that will only feed the fire.

The BSer

<u>Stretching—or Ignoring—the Truth</u>

Lies, lies, lies. Little white lies. Half-truths. Stretched truths. Exaggerations. Broken promises. All held to be harmless because—well—this is business, right?

It's interesting how the process of selling something (or marketing something or advertising something) seemingly empowers us all (most of us anyway) to embellish the truth—even just a little bit. We want to make our product, our service, our company sound better than the competition. We give ourselves the latitude to claim, "We're the best," even though there is no hard evidence to that effect.

A BSer in a negotiation stretches the truth (or, in the worst cases, ignores it altogether) to get what she wants. You may see this through your personal "lie detector." You may notice shifty eyes, broken voices (or extra firm voices) and feel that something just isn't right. What she says seems to be more what you want to hear than the truth; it just doesn't pass the smell test.

Recognizable Characteristics

Honed from experience, both in business and our personal lives, we all have our own personal BS detectors. Statements unsupported by facts or supported more by pomp and ebullience than facts are dead giveaways. Large quantities of superlatives can also tip you off—most, best, least, cheapest. Loss of eye contact, a change in a speech pattern, and general nervousness can all indicate a lie or exaggeration.

Some exaggeration and hyperbole indeed come with the business territory, particularly with gray areas that are difficult to support with facts. Our minds tend to wrap around our own products as best, and when we go into selling or evangelizing mode ourselves, it's natural to want others on our bandwagon. "Ours is the most beautiful on the road" isn't a lie, it's a matter of judgment—but if you hear too many such statements, look out.

Counteracting the BSer

The best way to counteract the BSer is to call her out by asking her to support her statements. Don't be bashful about this—simply state that getting the facts is vital for you to have proper confidence in the negotiation. If you call out the facts repeatedly, you'll make it clear that you're onto her style and ploy— particularly if you find she's repeatedly gotten the facts wrong.

The BSer tries to take control of the meeting and get the upper hand by fabricating ideas for you to swallow. If you swallow too many untruths and exaggerations, you open the door to more and more of them. It happens all the time in the business and personal world. Keep in mind, BS only works when you believe it. Simple advice: don't. Let your counterparty know early on that you're onto any lies, you will seek the truth even if it's uncomfortable, and that if she continues to bend the truth, you'll depart from the negotiation. You don't have time for this.

The Logical Thinker

<u>Analysis Paralysis</u>

Logical thinkers, naturally, can be quite reasonable to work with. However, in some cases, they tend to overanalyze issues and linger on them too long. They often nitpick and bring up valid points that you might acknowledge but not necessarily agree with. If you disagree, they probe your reasons why. If you do agree, that encourages them to probe some more.

The main problem with logical thinkers is that they create a lot of what should be "parking lot" discussions that sidetrack the negotiation through this constant questioning of details. (I call these "parking lot" discussions because they're the kind that should happen in the parking lot when you're all done with the main discussion and are getting ready to get in your car and leave.) The challenge is to keep focus and avoid going off into the weeds to overanalyze minor issues.

That said, all but the most detail-adverse negotiators typically like to work with logical thinkers. They are insightful and don't play emotional mind games to try to get you off course. They may derail you through their analysis and requests for detail, but this is a genuine part of their nature, not a negotiating tactic. If you satisfy their needs for detail, the win-win comes easier.

Recognizable Characteristics

The logical thinker deals with facts and figures. Most are naturally skeptical, and most ask a lot of questions, and they emphasize detail. Their questions may seem frivolous or beside the point to you, but they aren't logical thinking counterparty. The logical thinker is trying to draw conclusions, test the validity of your statements and claims, weed out inaccuracies, and evaluate information.

Occasionally you may run into a counterparty who isn't a logical thinker but who uses intense questioning and analysis to get you off balance or to "filibuster" a deal he doesn't want. You can usually recognize this ploy by the frivolity of the questions and whether he appears to be listening or responding to your answers.

Counteracting the Logical Thinker

The best way to deal with the logical thinker is to make every statement clear and back each up by sound research. Don't use jargon or statistics and facts you can't support. Be mindful that every person who asks a question isn't employing the logical thinker style of negotiating—you'll figure it out by the persistence of questions, the level of detail, and how the questioner responds to the answers. If he appears to be analyzing the facts and your answers to his questions, he fits the logical thinker mold.

Basically, you want to try to play his game. Satisfy his information needs. Be a logical thinker yourself—ask a lot of questions yourself and demand facts to back up assertions. The logical thinker will respond well to this. But at the same time, it's a good idea to assume leadership of the meeting, politely keep it on track and out of the weeds, and keep the agenda and the ultimate win-win deal front and center. Don't hesitate to take breaks when things go off track. You can discuss some of those nagging details during your break but come back ready to discuss the substantive topics on your agenda.

Negotiation Personalities

So far in this chapter, we've discussed negotiating styles—which, not surprisingly, are a function of an individual's personality. In this section, we'll take apart those styles to discover the specific building blocks of a negotiator's personality—the core elements of personality that are a part of someone's negotiating style.

Negotiating styles are chosen and developed by the individuals who deploy them, while negotiating personalities are innate; they are a natural and typically unchangeable part of someone's being. Just as you can recognize a negotiating style and deal with it over the table, you can also learn to recognize personalities. This section will help you do that. Armed with this knowledge, you can create a checklist of ways to deal with the different personalities. This section will also help you better understand your own negotiating personality. Finally, assessing your counterparty's negotiating personality during the preparation phase, if possible, will create a more effective negotiation.

I will cover six negotiating personalities:

- Aggressive/Dominating,
- Passive/Submissive,
- Logical/Analytical,
- Friendly/Collaborative,
- Evasive/Uncooperative,
- and Expressive/Communicative.

As you might surmise, a negotiator can exhibit more than one of these personalities.

Aggressive / Dominating

You've no doubt dealt with an aggressive personality. This personality is motivated by power and influence, and manifests itself in the following familiar traits:

- Demanding
- Pushy
- Bossy
- Self-centered
- Controlling
- Challenging
- Disdainful of weakness
- Rude
- Vengeful
- Easily angered
- Dominant
- Defensive
- Competitive
- Persistent
- Power junkie (enjoys the power and respects people in power)
- Forceful
- Intimidating
- Ambitious
- Successful
- Impatient
- Shrewd
- Fast learning

How they operate

Individuals with aggressive/dominating "driver" personalities tend to talk fast and act fast. They don't want to spend any more time with you than necessary. They're usually busy; they thrive in a fast-paced work environment. Preparing to negotiate with them means that you need to have all the facts in order beforehand and be ready for a speedy discussion. Their patience is in short supply; they will rush you along with every chance they get. For an aggressive/dominating individual, a negotiation becomes all about control pretty quickly.

As negotiators, aggressive personality types want to win as much as they can and give as little as possible. Victory is their main goal, and they're used to getting their own way. They may adopt a positional negotiating style, caring little for how you fare in the deal. When they don't get their way, they can become agitated and even more difficult to deal with.

<u>Playing defense</u>

"Fight fire with fire" may be one defensive tactic. Or you can try to slow them down by being cool, calm, and matter-of-fact. Adhering to a well-structured agenda can also help. Turning the floor over to someone else in the room or on a call can help, too. Be cool, play steady, avoid emotional responses, and stick to the facts and the win-win mantra.

Passive / Submissive

This personality is the exact opposite of the aggressive/dominating personality. Passive/submissive negotiators tend to exhibit the following characteristics:

- Nice, friendly
- Considerate
- Insecure
- Loner
- Calm
- Reserved
- Avoid being the center of attention
- Prefer to work alone or with a few people rather than in groups
- Obedient
- Quiet
- Uncomfortable with conflict
- Fear not being liked
- Sensitive
- Shy
- Introverted
- Good listener

How they operate

Passive/submissive negotiators are typically more focused on pleasing other people than on the mechanics of the negotiation itself. They are often taken advantage of but watch out. It's easy to misinterpret these attributes—an aggressive wolf can reside in sheep's clothing! Truly submissive negotiators want others to like them. They'll do whatever they can to make the other party happy, even if it means giving extra concessions or letting the other party renege on one of theirs. They are well suited to win-win negotiations, but they may be inclined to give up too much too early.

Submissive personalities seldom take control of the negotiation. They don't like the limelight, and they're more comfortable following than leading. They don't want to cause chaos or disturb the peace, so they rarely speak out of turn or voice their thoughts and opinions.

Watch Out for Passive-Aggressives

As a variant of submissive behavior, you might be dealing with passive-aggressive behavior, where calm, polite, or even reticent behavior masks more aggressive notions under the surface. Perhaps initially assessed as pushover behavior, such behavior may come back to bite you later in the negotiation or after the negotiation, and it can be hard to spot.

One tactic for discovering passive-aggressive behavior is to lay out a small task, a request, or an open issue within the negotiation. Let the counterparty take the item to research or decide on during the meeting and report back to you before the end. She typically will accept the item politely or with little response. When she gets back to you, assess the aggressiveness of her response. If she doesn't accomplish your request at all or does something different than what you asked, she probably falls into the passive-aggressive camp.

Playing defense

No defense is required, save for the passive-aggressive variant noted in the sidebar. When you see passive-aggressive behavior, switch into aggressive defense mode—stick to agendas, facts, and the common purpose of the negotiation. Don't give in to this behavior.

You may have to work to draw out the true needs or plan of a passive/submissive negotiator. Work hard to preserve the relationship so that you may get invited back for subsequent negotiations. Although you may be tempted to take advantage of a passive/submissive counterparty, resist doing so—win-win preserves the relationship and future negotiating opportunities.

Logical / Analytical

Analytical personalities tend to exhibit the following traits:

- Probing

- Apprehensive
- Mistrusting
- Fact-checker
- Even-keeled
- Thrive on information
- Thorough with details
- Take time with decisions
- Insensitive
- Logical
- Fair
- Firm
- Critical
- Thoughtful
- Organized
- Prepared
- Thinker
- Always early or on time

Logical/analytical negotiators must have all the facts, details, and information about the negotiation. They favor thorough preparation and have no desire to rush ahead.

How they operate

Analyzers like to solve problems and seek a deeper understanding of what they already know. They are achievers and have a strong sense of accomplishment

—that is more important to them than power in the negotiation. In fact, they seek to achieve power through knowledge and achievement, not through exhibitions of personality or hierarchy and credentials.

Expect logical/analytical personalities to walk into the meeting room armed with data and facts. You may feel like you're closely scrutinized during the discussion as if you're under a microscope. The counterparty seeks errors and inconsistencies in your presentation. This may come across as overcritical, but logical analyzers typically seek comfort in covering all bases before deciding. You should prepare by knowing the facts and by being ready to research them on the fly if necessary.

Playing Defense

It's simple—be prepared. When possible, have documentation to back up your materials. Prepared graphs, charts, slides, and reports can all help. Don't bluff, stretch the truth, skew the facts, or tell half-truths—you're likely to be discovered. Prepare to be on trial. Try to help your counterparty get his facts together, draw conclusions, and make decisions (he may need help with the latter!).

A slight pressure can go a long way

Logical/analytical negotiators often take a long time to make decisions. They tend to be a little insecure with their facts; they feel as if there's one more element to be explored. Try to reassure them and feather in a little push or two along the way to help them get through their analysis and work toward the close. Left to their own devices, they might never do that.

Friendly / Collaborative

The one most of us like best—the friendly and collaborative negotiator—is easy to recognize:

- Fair
- Courteous
- Empathetic
- Tactful
- Warm
- Friendly
- Successful
- Open-minded
- Resourceful
- Sincere
- Patient
- General concern for others
- Considerate
- Appreciative

- Understanding
- Honest
- Ability to employ creative thinking techniques
- Flexible
- Sensitive
- Tolerant
- Character and integrity

Such friendly/collaborative negotiators possess the principles needed to reach win-win solutions. They understand that a negotiation is not a battle. Instead, it's an opportunity to attain mutual success with the least amount of resistance and negativity.

<u>How they operate</u>

Collaborators are concerned with working toward results quickly and with everyone's agreement. They want to build trust and develop solid relationships for the future. They try to learn as much as possible about their counterparties and their objectives so that the desired outcome can be achieved.

You're in luck when negotiating with a collaborator. You'll recognize the warm smile and friendly bearing. She listens and listens well. But don't be fooled—these negotiators possess a keen business sense and, at day's end, place the importance of task above you and above the relationship. They are true professionals.

Another wolf?

Earlier I described the passive-aggressive personality. A quiet and polite demeanor might be mistaken for submissive behavior. Sometimes, though, this is a wolf in sheep's clothing, as this quiet personality will agitate to undermine the negotiation or ignore your requests and agreements sometime down the road.

A similar wolf can wear the disguise of an outwardly friendly and cohesive personality. This wolf waits until you become comfortable—too comfortable—and then pounces. If you have been to a car dealer, chances are you have seen this behavior in action. They show you around, let you test drive the car, answer all your questions; they're your best friend. Then suddenly, they open their drawer, grab a sales contract form, and start talking monthly payments—so much for your comfort! This sort of behavior is collaborative to a point. And at the point where you get sucked in, the negotiating fireworks begin. Don't be oversold on a counterparty's apparent friendly and collaborative nature.

Playing defense

No defense is really necessary—except to make sure the behavior is genuine, not forced. To test this, you might throw an unreasonable request her way to see how she deals with it. If things suddenly become confrontational, then "collaborator" probably isn't her true personality. Be honest in your dealings with a genuinely friendly/collaborative negotiator so that your counterparty sees you as being collaborative, too.

Evasive / Uncooperative

Some negotiators will seem reluctant to negotiate or even to be there at all. These negotiators tend to exhibit the following characteristics:

- Insecure
- Fearful
- Careful
- Calm
- Reserved
- Procrastinator
- Nonresponsive
- Cold
- Pessimistic
- Easily embarrassed
- Play it safe
- Don't like confrontation
- Introverted
- Timid
- Indifferent

Evasive/uncooperative negotiators deal with issues—
or people—by disregarding them altogether. It's not
that they don't want to succeed; they either don't
know how to or are reluctant to get involved out of
disinterest or weakness. Some may be wolves in
sheep's clothing as well, playing the passive-aggressive
card to get what they want by not giving you what
you want during the discussion.

How they operate

Evasive/uncooperative negotiators seek to endure the
negotiation without losing. They may be personally
insecure or may not feel prepared or knowledgeable
about the topic being negotiated. Lack of cooperation
and silence for them are survival techniques to avoid
saying anything that might be uncomfortable or
weaken their position. Or, once again, it can be part of
a ploy to gain control through passive-aggressive
behavior.

It's easy to get frustrated with this negotiating type as
he tends to postpone discussions and withhold or
delay critical information. Issues go unresolved; you
may feel that nothing much is being accomplished.
Communication may break down or become tense.

Playing defense

This personality type is difficult; you must diagnose
the cause. If the driver is insecure, try to draw the

negotiator out of his shell by reaching out to him and by helping him overcome his fear. If your counterparty has passive-aggressive tendencies, focus on the need to get the task done and make a few concessions to offer some sense of control. Don't withdraw or withhold information yourself; that just keeps the cycle going and may postpone the arrival at a successful outcome forever.

Expressive / Communicative

Expressive negotiators exhibit the following traits:

- Playful
- Spontaneous
- Charming
- Self-involved
- A "people person"
- Open
- Easily distracted
- Short attention span
- Energetic
- Talkative
- Sociable
- Enthusiastic
- Think out loud
- Extroverted

- Like being the center of attention
- Ambitious
- Not a good listener
- Like to be reassured

Expressive/communicative negotiators are generally very animated and convey a fun-loving attitude in most situations. They enjoy their work, crave attention, and thrive on rapport. They want to get the negotiation done, feel like they've won, and believe they've entertained you along the way.

How They Operate

Aside from becoming your new best friend, the expressive/communicative negotiators seek to get the most out of the deal by using their social skills and optimism. As such, they may take it personally when you disagree or reject one of their offers. The discussion tends to center on them, sometimes more than the topic being negotiated, and your response and attention—as well as your willingness to do things their way—is their reward.

Instead of conducting business in an even, businesslike tone, expressive/communicative negotiators turn the negotiation into a social function. They may jump from one topic to the next and may be hard to pin down on a particular item. At times they may not let you get a word in edgewise.

Playing Defense

The best way to work with expressive/communicative negotiators is to allow them to do their thing, at least in the beginning. This helps you build rapport. Then, try to keep the negotiation on task with well-timed questions and a focus on the agenda. Don't let them jump around, and don't let them do too much schmoozing. Avoid being too consumed by their charm.

Dealing with difficult personalities

Let's face it—we don't get along with everybody, and some people who we have to deal with just flat out rub us the wrong way. What can you do when you just don't mesh well with your counterparty?

The best approach—and I've mentioned this a few times in the Playing Defense subsections—is to try to ignore the unpleasant aspects of your counterparty's personality or style. If he's loud and aggressive, don't respond; stick to business and a normal level of aplomb for the situation. If he's evasive and passive-aggressive, don't take the bait.

Second, and related—stick to business. Focus on the task at hand, on the problem, not the people. Stick to the facts, stick to the agenda. This is part of why it's so important to come prepared with the facts and a plan.

Finally, use the clock effectively. Take time-outs to regroup or to ease the tension. You can use those breaks from the negotiation table to establish some informal rapport with your counterparty to diminish some of your differences (which is often easier done in a friendlier, less pressured situation).

The bottom line—and I can't stress it enough—is preparation. Visualize the negotiation, including your response to the problematic personalities you may encounter. And be prepared to separate the people from the problem.

Define your own negotiation style

Which of the following best describes your negotiating style: collaborative, competitive, or compromising? When defining goals and showing your negotiating personality, you're likely to discover your negotiating style during any professional negotiation skills training.

But, if you're having problems answering that question, you're not alone. This is because good negotiators generally adopt all of these approaches throughout a negotiation:

• They pay great attention and work together to produce value.

• They compete to see who can get the biggest piece of the pie.

- When required, they make compromises.

In negotiating skills training, putting labels on negotiation styles can be a mistake. When I used to teach negotiation, I would educate my students on the most prevalent negotiation styles, discuss their merits, and then encourage them to develop their negotiation abilities so that they could draw on several types as a negotiation unfolded.

In contrast, rather than discussing the usefulness of different methods, I now introduce students to the negotiating abilities that underpin the various negotiation styles. Rather than educating students about different negotiating approaches, negotiation teachers should push them to develop five specific abilities.

- Assertiveness
- Empathy
- Flexibility
- Social abilities or intuition
- Ethics

Adult professionals learn more effectively when they first discuss their experiences and talents before focusing on framework or style selection.

Labeling negotiating styles – distributive, integrative, problem-solving, conciliatory, and so on – might help us learn broad distinctions in how people view and behave during negotiations. Labels also assist negotiating researchers in organizing their ideas around a common language.

However, naming negotiation styles can be problematic in negotiation skills training.

Suppose a student is taught that an integrative (or value-creating or collaborative) negotiating style is superior to a distributive (or value-claiming or competitive) negotiating style. In that case, they may struggle to understand why both value creation and value-claiming behaviors are beneficial in negotiation.

Furthermore, the categories used to characterize diverse negotiating styles do not cleanly transfer onto negotiation skills. A warm manner and a strong sense of justice might help a highly competitive negotiator defy the stigma of this approach. In addition, many negotiation techniques taught in the classroom, such as researching criteria to back up fairness claims, can be employed in both competitive and collaborative circumstances.

Chapter Six

TECHNIQUES AND TACTICS IN NEGOTIATION

C aught in the vortex of confrontations and quarrels, we control our impulsive reactions with difficulty. Suppose we use several tactics, techniques, tricks and negotiation schemes already learned and practiced; the chances of keeping the control increase considerably. They help us to take over the initiative but also to recognize the opponent's tactics to administer the proper antidote. If we discover the opponent's techniques, we tear apart some of its power of negotiation. In addition, we have at hand a deliberate tactic line, a plan that deserves to be respected. Our negotiating power increases as we assimilate negotiation schemes validated both by theory and practice. There are hundreds of such tactics and techniques both in diplomacy and in business.

Before proceeding to other theoretical and practical considerations, we will present a collection of tactics and negotiation techniques offered under concentrated pills.

Useful recommendations in negotiating

• Before negotiating, you should document as thoroughly as possible. The time used for documentation is extremely rewarded.

• Establish your priorities and rank them.

• Start in force, give up slowly. Aim high, creating the margin of negotiation and making small and slow concessions. Always make sure that the opponent makes concessions.

• During the negotiation, try to keep a balance between both your interests and your partner's. It is not sure that you will get a maximum of results through a tough and uncompromising position and, in addition, you can turn the other person into a personal enemy. A transaction is not mandatory to have winners and losers. If the business is properly conducted, both sides can win. Even more: most of the time, if the other party doesn't win anything, if it hasn't a real interest in making the respective transaction, you will lose, too, no matter how good a negotiator you are.

• Focus on your core interests. Do not miss the interests with which you started the negotiation.

These are the really important ones, not the positions taken during negotiations. Pride is a good thing sometimes, but sometimes not. It depends on the cases. Adjust your strategy to fit the situation.

• Compare the offers you receive in the course of negotiations with alternatives you have if you don't reach an agreement. Do not stick with various unrealistic objectives you set for yourself. On the other hand, an empty stomach is not a good political adviser.

• Consider the short-term and long-term advantages. Sometimes it can be more convenient to settle for something less if you get the certainty of long-term gains, with the condition that it is indeed a fact.

• As a negotiator, your position should always vary between honesty, discretion and misinformation. In negotiation, there are very few situations in which you can afford to be completely open and honest without risking being exploited. On the other hand, if you don't give any information, you risk creating so much distrust that you will lose the negotiation partner.

• Pay attention to the feelings of those with whom you do business. If you offend or humiliate them, this might hang more than anything else when they are in a position to make a decision. If they don't have the chance to return it immediately, they will wait for the right moment to pay it back. People never forget personal offenses.

• During negotiations, ask as many questions as possible. With questions, you can discover your opponent's real targets to get information; you can avoid conflicts and can convince.

• Do not get overwhelmed by the pressure of time. Your deadlines, if known, can be used by the opponent. Display a lot of patience and make an ally of the time.

• Listen carefully. Prove that you understand what your discussion partner says by repeating his words.

• Affirm your goals. To do this, choose the correct and appropriate words and gestures that convey power and authority, but don't be aggressive.

• Offer short proposals at the conditional mode. When you receive a proposal, do not make counter-proposals in your turn and do not use the word "no."

• Multiply the variables of negotiation.

• Check what was agreed. Never leave the negotiating table without you reviewing each point of the agreement. Summarize each item in writing and determine how to resolve disputes.

• Build long-term relationships. Prove the other party that he can rely on you, that you are rational and responsive. Seek ways so that both of you win at last and try the satisfaction of both parties. Be constructive.

• Analyze what you have done. Learn from past mistakes. Review in mind the negotiations that have just ended and look for areas where you can improve your negotiating attitude.

Avoid saying NO

Say NO as rarely as possible! Diplomats say "no" almost never. As good negotiators from around the world, they learned this from Asians. Marco Polo wrote that he met their real schools where ambassadors and spokespersons of Mongol princes and Tibetan were trained back from his long journey in Asia. They received in the evening the exact same number of rods on the sole as the number of "NO" delivered by their lips that day.

People hate to be negative, contested, contradicted. "No" is a direct and categorical denial that cut, tear and strikes. "NO" irritates and disturbs. It lacks delicacy. Tactfully people avoid it carefully. Expressed simply, clearly and unequivocally, the negation "NO" runs out of options. It leaves no return. Plus, it breaks the communication. Instead, phrases like "Yeah ... but ..." can be used in the sense of negation, keeping the other two types of options. It has three possible aspects: one that is "Yes," one that means "maybe," and another which means "No." Why say "no" when there is "yes ... but ..."? This is welcome in almost any situation. You will agree regarding a commander's reaction after receiving such a response, even if the answer is argued.

More elegant is, for example: "Yes, I will resolve the situation but ..." and only after that "but" will follow a logical sequence of arguments that will demonstrate step by step that he is unable to execute the order. The secret of the formula "yes, but" is that it allows formulating other people's opinions as a sequel to what the commandant said and not as a direct contradiction of it.

False offers tactic - in short, it can be characterized as a bargaining trick that involves some theater acting. In general, price negotiation is a game in which one cannot win without losing the other. If possible, opponents manipulate between them, even to the limit of loyalty and morality.

One of the unfair tactics, rarely found in textbooks and often in practice, is that the buyer makes an attractive offer to the seller to eliminate the competition and motivate the transaction's development. Once obtained it, he finds a reason to modify the initial offer. Then they start the discussion through which he tries to convince the seller to accept a new offer, usually more moderate. Often, the seller is forced to no longer have a choice.

Stress and nag

Another tactic often used by great negotiators is to stress and nag. This strategy weakens the physical and mental strength of the opponent. Many kinds of maneuvers can be used, although they are not directly insulting and humiliating. They serve to annoy the opponent, putting him in a position to hasten the end of the negotiations. You can easily find ways of harassing and stressing.

For example, take him for a prolonged walk inside the unit. You can accommodate him in a room exposed to the noise that would prevent him from sleeping. He can be placed with his eyes in the sun or other irritating light source at the negotiating table. It can also be placed on a comfortable armchair only in appearance, which, apart from being luxurious, squeaks, so the caller will be forced to sit still.

The examples may continue, but remember that these are methods to be applied only in extreme cases. When we are not interested in long-term relationships and intend to use such means of pressure, these maneuvers must be made under the guise of the most exquisite innocent and helpful appearance, asking for excuses and pretending to be victims along with our opponent.

Bribery method

Another tactic, quite simple to use but unfortunately common in almost any environment, is the bribery method. Totally unfair, it is based on weakening the opponent's psychological resistance put in a position to accept small or large gifts. This tactic is favored when negotiations are conducted through insufficiently motivated intermediaries by the party they represent.

There is a significant difference between protocol and gift, on the one hand, and bribery, on the other hand. There are some similarities, though. The role of protocol and gift is to induce favorable behavior towards the person that offers it. The little attention placed on the negotiating table like pens, calendars, key chains, coffee or drinks are, to a certain level, absolutely natural and are designed to create a favorable environment for negotiators. Long-term business relationships can be compromised by bribes but favored by large gifts. The difference between gift and bribery is psychological and strategic.

Time pressure tactics are based on the idea that negotiators always have a negotiation program and a schedule to keep their meetings. For this purpose, you can use any tricks and maneuvers to delay and postpone it. Towards the end of negotiations, things usually start to precipitate. Of course, one of the discussion partners will be pressed by some problems that do not require postponement. The discussion pace should be rushed and, then, the opponent can easily commit errors.

When asking too much, sometimes, the opponent may feel overwhelmed and may refuse us at first. He finds it much easier to respond with a refusal. For him, it becomes more difficult to play the game without making concessions under too much pressure. Instead, we can reach a safe and complete victory by getting repeated partial benefits, armed with patience and tact. Small successes may go unnoticed but may be added, resulting in considerable time achievements. We don't have to find ourselves in possession of the entire salami so we can eat him.

Common tactics

Alternating negotiators' tactics adhere to the idea that you have to start everything over again when the partner switches the negotiator. The first version of this tactic makes the negotiating team leader look really gentle and reasonable but totally helpless in front of his team of specialists. In a deliberate and premeditated prolonged way, the other team members are tough, stubborn and seemingly irresponsible.

During the negotiations, people from teams with various specialties are introduced, in turn, in order to display a hard and uncompromising position. In this way, they create psychological pressure on the opponent. This is why he prefers to work only with the team leader and accept his more reasonable proposals. The second version of this tactic is the effective change of the negotiator. It can be a hard and unexpected strike which one can deal with difficulty because it is not nice to take all over again.

The new negotiator can raise new arguments, revoke some of the agreements already made, or withdraw concessions from his predecessor. The new negotiator is usually the top man that takes you for granted when your predecessor hasn't already exhausted you. In these cases, it is better to adapt to the new situation and not get tired by repeating old arguments and modifying your attitude according to the new negotiator. If you climbed up here, there is no use in backing down now.

"Put the foot in" tactics is a minor psychological manipulation technique. You want to snatch a privilege, a concession, an agreement. For this, you influence his thoughts, feelings and behavior in your favor. People manipulate each other in the most natural way possible. The baby, who whimpers or caresses his mother to receive a toy, manipulates her in the most innocent method and from his natural instinct. To a lesser extent, a gift or some flowers may be handling tools in the positive sense of the word.

There are some major manipulation techniques like neuro-linguistic programming and hypnosis or a lot of minor handling simple techniques used in negotiations, as in everyday human relations. To cause someone to make a major concession, you first dig your foot in, so that the door remains ajar. You ask for something insignificant but at the same time hard to get. Only after that, you elicit the real request, which was taken into account from the beginning.

"Good guy - bad guy" is a good tactic for employers and union negotiations. The title is the name of tactics used with excellent results in wage negotiations. It is borrowed from detective films and experiences with long interrogations, where the suspect is passed from one investigator to another. It is also found in textbooks.

The "deliberate errors" tactics. Its motto is: "Forgive my involuntary mistake, partner!" People are humans, and making mistakes involves being human. The good Samaritan knows this, and he often forgives others' mistakes. In business, this general principle is sometimes used as an unfair bargaining tactic. Some deliberately "go wrong" and even long premeditated, with the express purpose to confuse and deceive. Deliberate mistakes slip in written documents, in reports, in Annex, in addenda etc.

Most often, deliberate errors have as purpose replacing certain words with others that bring additional advantages without exaggerating: "net profit" by "gross profit"; "inclusive VAT" by "exclusive VAT"; "with adding" through "without adding" etc. Many traders know the tactic of deliberate errors, and this is why it's better to check twice before you sign once.

The "hostage" technique. In more veiled forms, the hostage tactics are found in various aspects of daily life and, of course, in business negotiations. It is ugly and immoral, but it does not prevent it from being effective. Typically, the hostage tactics dress the sordid coat of blackmailing. The "hostage" does not have to be a person. It can be a document, information, a situation, a good amount of money or anything important enough to force the opponent's hand. The rule is simple: the hostage is "captured" and held "captive" until the opponent pays a "reward" or makes a "concession" that would not be done under normal conditions. Reward or concession can be excessive, but the alternative is even worse.

The "shutting the door against someone" technique. According to this technique, to increase the chances of getting some favor from someone, we first ask for another more important favor, but at the same time knowing that we will almost certainly be refused. Only after the refusal, when we have slammed the door in the face, we come back with the request that we had in mind from the beginning. The chances of getting what we want to grow considerably.

Statistical "intoxication." In most cases, the immediate and practical purpose of a negotiation tactic is to convince your opponent that you are right, possibly without directly contradicting him. To this end, he may be besieged and bombarded with all kinds of statistics: studies extracts from the press, selection of books, booklets, brochures, offers, catalogs etc., which serve exclusively to your own point of view. The rule is simple: never and nothing to support the opposite view.

The surprise tactic. In negotiation, the surprise and alternating rhythm tactics are based on unpredictable reasoning or negotiating parties' behavior. Sudden and unexpected hijacking of direction in the discussion, silences and surprising interruptions, the launch of arguments and unexpected advantages etc., can have a bemusing effect and continuously intimidate the opponent, weakening its ability to react. You get patiently closer to the agreement and then move away to get close again, etc. The opponent will oscillate between hope and renunciation. The surprise tactic can give good results against inexperienced or poorly trained negotiators who learn these negotiating schemas by heart. When they are suddenly removed from the script prepared in advance, they remain confused and rush to reach some agreement to finish everything quickly.

"Time out" technique. Periodic interruption of the negotiation process by requesting "time out" may be a way to temper an irritable partner or fragment and disrupt an argument. In addition, the request of a break when the opponent launches an attack or forces the obtaining of an unacceptable concession may be useful to prepare a satisfactory defense, document for consultation, and formulate a strategy to counterattack. In addition, the "time-out" can pull your opponent out of his hand, cutting the offensive impulses.

The "short-circuit" tactic. Sometimes we can be brought face to face with a very difficult negotiator. It either possesses a psychological dominance that we do not like or is in a position of strength and adversity. Plus, they might be highly skilled specialists in the issue of interest. The only solution that can save us in such cases is to avoid the difficult human. This is sometimes possible by raising the level of the negotiations at a higher hierarchical rank. This is called short-circuit.

Paraphrase technique. In negotiations, paraphrasing means to summarize what you understood from what the partner said in your own words. The fact that it involves his own view should be mentioned explicitly. The paraphrase is introduced simply by sentences like: "If I understand well ..." or "Let's see if I understood what you mean ..." or "You mean ...". With a paraphrase, we ask for further clarifications. By paraphrasing, we easily get the chance to have further clarifications.

The "questions" technique. Both questions and answers are a part of the negotiation process. As Aristotle was saying, "the questioner leads." Any question has the character of a request, and the answer is a concession. The art of formulating questions and answers does not involve being right or wrong but knowing what and how to tell, what and how not to say. In any case, a good negotiator knows most of the questions and answers that will be enunciated before actually sitting down at the negotiating table. He behaves like a student who masters the subject and cannot be confused by the teacher.

With well-formulated questions, you can always take the initiative. You can check and clarify the opponent's statements. You can check if certain suspicions regarding the opponent's attitude are grounded through questions you already know the answer to. Even if we get the agreement, the partner may often call the "trick" to ask for one last concession. By doing so, he can get us mad. But all we can do in order to avoid an eventual evil is ask a question like: "Are you suggesting reopening?" If he answers no, what remains to do is to respect the terms of the agreement already negotiated. If so, he will be asked for another concession in return.

Seven keys to becoming a Master Negotiator

The difference between sitting down at the negotiation table and bargaining effectively is comparable to the difference between a ballplayer who simply shows up and one who shows up prepared to play. That's why all good negotiators (and ballplayers) put on their game face. This skilled negotiator offers sound guidance that will prepare any manager to play to win.

According to my observations, the most successful negotiators, those whose track record qualifies them as master negotiators, employ seven distinct methods.

Strategy #1: Strengthen your bargaining power

You have to have something to offer. You have to have something of value to begin with because your counterparts' perception of your starting hand plays a big role in how they shape their negotiating position. If they feel that you have very little to offer, expect stiff resistance.

On the other hand, if you have a very compelling starting hand, don't be surprised if they come off as initially more accommodating.

Strategy #2: Set the logistics

Taking the initiative to coordinate how you're going to meet, where you're going to meet when you're going to meet, and other crucial terms enable you to pre-qualify the other party.

They can see that you're in command. They can see that you're serious.

Strategy #3: Focus on building rapport

Make sure you establish mutual comfort. This leads to you seeing eye to eye and establishing that you're not necessarily in the same room to beat each other up or gain an unfair advantage over each other.

This takes the adversarial air out of the negotiations and enables people to drill down to the stuff that really matters instead of wasting precious energy and time on brinksmanship.

Strategy #4: Be in the right mood

You can't have a poker face during negotiations, and you have to have the right emotions on your face because your emotions influence the final resolution of the negotiation.

Strategy #5: Be the first to make the offer

When you take the initiative in making the offer, you set the tone and the range of the negotiation. The negotiation starts to work around the first move you made, and this gives you the upper hand.

Strategy #6: Frame a win-win offer

Make sure you package or position your offer in such a way that it's obvious that the other side and your party will win from your offer. Do not position it as an "I win, you lose" offer, and this makes the offer more palatable and easier to live with to the other party.

Strategy #7: Be ready to counter their offer

The worst thing you can do is to get caught flat-footed when the other side makes a counteroffer to your offer. It may be a very generous offer, or at least seem like it. These are the most dangerous.

It makes you think that they've given in. It turns out you probably would've gotten a much better deal. So get ready to counter their offer, whatever it is.

Improve your bargaining power

You have to strengthen your bargaining power before negotiations. This is a powerful way of pre-qualifying the other party. If they are under the impression that you really don't have much to offer or the value you seek to offer is not really all that high, don't be surprised that they lowball you.

It wouldn't be too shocking if they put up a wall because you don't really have much to offer in their head. Either they can get it from somewhere else, or the intrinsic value of what you have to offer really isn't that compelling.

Great negotiators do a good job selling the other side first before they negotiate. One way to do this is to say, "This deal is a miracle because I've got 5 other people lining up for this property. They need it immediately, and despite my busy schedule, I decided to call you and see what you think. I know that you are interested in this property as well. So I figured in fairness because you approached me first to hear your offer."

Pay attention to what I just said. Do you see the value that you put in your offer? Do you see how you position whatever it is you're selling or whatever it is you possess in the eyes of the other party?

The key here is value. Put more precisely, we're talking about perceived value. You see, when it comes to negotiations, perception is reality. Little do they know that the five people who spoke to you about the property may not be all that excited about it, and they just want to price out the neighborhood.

Maybe they are interested, but they're not ready to buy right now. You just have to say, "Several people approached me about this property."

The key is to control the perception of value. When you say those things, what do you trigger? That's right. You trigger the all too human fear of scarcity. Thousands of years ago, our ancestors were walking through savannas. These are grasslands in Africa.

So when they see a game animal, maybe it's a wildebeest or some sort of buffalo or zebra, they kill it because they know that the next time they eat may be days, if not weeks, from now.

This scarcity mindset has been seared into human DNA. No matter how cool the negotiator across the table from your may appear, they will have that scarcity DNA. When you say, "There are lots of people who are interested in this property, but I'm talking to you first," you trigger that.

A variation of this is, "I just got through a job interview with your biggest competitor, and I just wanted to interview with you because I'd like to know more about your company." Again, you're triggering the scarcity mindset because, at the back of their heads, they're thinking, "I better jump on this now because somebody else might get it."

This mindset is not so much different from an early caveman thinking, "I better eat this game animal now; otherwise, it'll be gone tomorrow. Who knows when I'll eat next?" Do you see the power of qualification? You have to come off with a perception of value.

Tap the power of BATNA

You can enhance your bargaining power to play up your BATNA, also known as the best alternative to a negotiated agreement. Before you negotiate, you have to research the other options available to you just in case your upcoming negotiation falls apart.

Not only will this give you other options and make you feel more confident coming into the negotiations, but it also gives you facts to share with your counterpart. When you're exploring your BATNA, you may run into alternative offers.

You may get other valuations. You may see other opportunities. This is very important on both a subjective basis (what's going on in your head and your moods) as well as on an objective basis. On an objective basis, when you explore your BATNA, you end up appraising the value of the asset or the resource you're negotiating over. This means that you know what you're representing and what you're standing on, which in turn pumps up your motivation to negotiate for its full value. There's this strong interplay between objective validation and subjective encouragement. When you come in, you don't give out the perception that you have a weak card. You know the value of what you bring to the table, and your counterpart can sense your confidence.

This is how BATNAs enhance your bargaining power. It is a form of pre-qualification. In a study published in a journal of applied psychology in April 2005, researchers measured the impact of BATNA on contribution when it comes to negotiator performance.

Contribution is when one party values the negotiation based on what they can add to the deal, and they look at what they can contribute. In the study of 140 business school graduate students, participants were asked how they would like to distribute profits and what would be acceptable to them. It turns out that the graduate students who were assigned greater BATNA are quite impressive when negotiations begin. This is because BATNA tends to pre-qualify participants before negotiations really proceed. But interestingly enough, as the negotiations proceed because of areas for bargaining like negotiating a profit distribution and who will do what, the more people can bargain, the weaker inherently superior BATNA becomes.

This study highlights the point that people have strong initial bargaining power thanks to BATNA. They shouldn't be too quick to bargain to diminish their initial strong hand. In other words, if you're going to come into a negotiation, emphasize the strength of your position.

Emphasize your BATNA.

This would then qualify the other side so you can get to a better deal. Otherwise, if you just go straight to negotiation and just downplay the BATNA you have, don't be surprised if you end up with a less than optimal deal.

The key takeaway here is to be as transparent with your BATNA as possible. Make it shine. This will let the other party know that you bring a good deal. So they better step up with their best deal.

Similarly, in a 2009 study in the journal of applied psychology, 198 volunteers were observed to determine the relationship between how straightforward negotiators are and the concessions they're likely to make.

The study participants were initially asked to fill out a questionnaire that measured how straightforward they were and also paid attention to certain personality traits that they may have.

After they had filled out the questionnaires, they would then be assigned to different role-playing groups, and each was given a room. One role-playing group is the pinnacle, and the other is the mountain.

These different groups were then asked to represent either the pinnacle or the mountain company. They're supposed to negotiate with each other to come to an agreement regarding seven issues involving how much money employees would be paid and the management of human resources.

The different pairings were given up to 45 minutes to negotiate on the seven issues. The outcomes of the negotiations are then recorded. Researchers then cross-reference the negotiated outcomes with the personality profiles of the participants.

In other words, if you're straightforward, you're more likely to get concessions from the other side than if you were playing it sly or you're trying to hide your agenda.

If they perceive you as a straight shooter, they're more likely to concede in exchange for a concession from you in the hopes of getting a win-win situation.

On the other hand, if they don't see you as straightforward, they're less likely to give an inch.

Step by step process for strengthening your initial bargaining power

Step #1: Identify and improve your BATNA

Are there better job offers in this industry or another industry if you're looking for a job? This takes quite a bit of research.

Instead, they will grind you down and say, "Well, you don't really have much to offer. So we'll lowball you." Don't let that happen by being clear about your BATNA and working hard to improve it.

By improving, it really all boils down to positioning. You may have a profoundly weak product. But that's not a death sentence in of itself. You can package it or bundle it with other products. You can partner with others. You can get a review.

Step #2: Identify and zero in on your counterpart's BATNA

If you have a BATNA, the other side has a BATNA as well. You have to do your research here. They're not going to tell you. Maybe they want to buy your company because they want to sell the combined company later.

They may have the cash, but they know that the handwriting is on the wall as far as their company's product maturity or service life trajectory goes. Whatever the case may be, their large-scale operation has a limited life of high profitability. So they're exploring their options.

Knowing this enables you to reposition your BATNA. Don't be afraid to ask questions at this point. Ask people within the organization, ask people in the industry, do your research, get white papers, get research reports, request annual reports or public filings.

There's a reason why they're talking to you. And frequently, it's not because you're weak and they're strong. They need you, and that's why they're talking to you. Otherwise, they probably wouldn't be talking to you right here, right now.

Step #3: Show the other party's BATNA in the worst light possible

After you've done your research about the other party's motivations as well as their options, show them your perception of their position in the worst light possible without being insulting.

For example, suppose you're a manufacturer and your negotiation with an importer with a domestic supplier of raw materials. In that case, they can tell you that they are the best domestic producer of the raw material you're looking for.

They will tell you that the material they provide is crucial to your product. Your product simply won't be as good without its raw materials. Fair enough. But you then tell them that you can easily import raw material of the same or superior quality from China at half the price.

When you do this, you just effectively destroy their BATNA. They're not as confident anymore. In fact, you send them into a tailspin, and they are more likely to re-evaluate the value that they bring to the table, which can play into your hands.

You can say, "Well, I can do that. But if I get a good deal with you, I'll stick with the domestic producer because I'd like to stay away from importing and just go with domestic production. After all, it's faster and more efficient." You probably already know the reasons to give them.

The key here is to weaken the other party's BATNA, so they're not as confident, which prepares you for the next step.

Step #4: Deliver a firm and confident request

After you weaken the other party's BATNA and play up your BATNA, you then deliver your request. The key here is to not crush the other side. If it's obvious that you're basically just lowballing and you're just being unreasonable, you make it easy for them to step away. You basically would say, "This person has just lowballed us, and this is not even in the ballpark." So, either you're not serious, or you're playing games. That's all they need to step out.

There is a fine line between showing dominance, which means you know that they know you have the upper hand. That's why your offer looks the way it does. This is very different from just being mean, being abusive and just being obnoxious. Know the difference.

Because when you're dominant, you can position the deal closer to your target price or target outcome. You're not being dominant when you walk away with empty hands because you overplayed your hand. So don't overplay your hand. It's one thing to show dominance, and it's another to just be completely obnoxious.

Chapter Seven

BODY LANGUAGE IN NEGOTIATIONS

U nderstanding body language begins with observing modes of behavior. Observation requires an objective registration of behavior. The observer shall have full availability in mood because if he is overwhelmed by his emotions, he cannot successfully perform these observations. He who wants to observe carefully has to be tolerant. We often minimalize the role of non-verbal cues and perceive only the tip of the iceberg in a conversation in which both partners have their own needs, desires, expectations, and aspirations.

Non-verbal language can support, contradict, or even replace verbal communication. A non-verbal message is closest to the issuer's reality, and it is the one that has the most attention from the partner. This is why we often find that although the party argues that he is telling the truth, we "feel" that he is lying. What is the "sixth sense" that receives the non-verbally expressed information from the issuer? It is believed that women have developed this "sixth sense" better than men. Experts in the field have established the following report on information perception by the receiver in oral communication:

- 7% words

- 38% - paralanguage (mainly intonation and inflection of voice)

- 55% - body language.

Non-verbal communication refers to the transmission of meaning through appearance, gestures, facial expressions, posture, movement, voice inflection, intonation, look, clothing, and so on. Body language helps communication through facial expression, body movements, posture, general appearance, and tactile communication.

Facial expression

A lot of meaning comes from minor changes in the orientation of the face. For example, a frowning forehead might signify concern, anger, or frustration; raised eyebrows with eyes open might signify surprise or wonder; tight lips might signify uncertainty, hesitation, or hiding information. A smile is a very complex gesture that can express a wide range of information, from pleasure, joy, and satisfaction to promise, cynicism, or embarrassment. Laughter, which is the limited response of a single behavior that reflects inner feelings, is an expression valid only to human beings. Laughter releases internal tension. The analysis of sounds in laughter indicated that laughter might contain one of the following vowels:

• A – open laughter from the heart; it is typical for honest people

• E – this is a burst of ugly laughter, almost onomatopoeic; it is the expression of mocking, contempt, and scorn

• I – this is the laughter of people who want to seem younger; it is an ironic laughter

• O - this kind of laughter corresponds to some tense reactions; it is a defense from an individual that experienced something negative; depending on the sound intensity, it can express anger, protest, and hatred

Looking at someone confirms that we recognize their presence, and intercepting one's gaze indicates a desire to communicate. A look can mean direct honesty or intimacy, but it can also carry common threats in some cases. In general, an insistent and continuous look bothers the person being regarded. Short flashes of contact often indicate friendliness. Looking to one side or avoiding looking directly at someone can denote a lack of interest or coldness. Avoiding someone else's gaze means hidden feelings, discomfort, or guilt. Dilated pupils indicate strong emotions. Pupils widen, in general, at the sight of something pleasant or something to which we have an attitude of sincerity. Pupils narrow as an expression of displeasure. Frequent blinking indicates anxiety. The specialists divided the human faces into six major types:

• Square type – considered to be energetic and active; has the will to achieve; authoritarian; conceited.

• Rectangular – needs work and domination, but it is more theoretical and shows less force in realizing ideas.

• Long face – hypersensitive; pessimistic; meditative.

• Triangulation – cerebral; bold; original; adventurous; imaginative; unstable.

• Round - has a hot temper; sanguine; cheerful; optimistic; with transient sorrows.

Body movement

In literature, seven main groups of facial expressions were established, although each group has many variations. These expressions include happiness, surprise, fear, sadness, anger, curiosity, disgust, or contempt. These groups appear to represent facial expressions recognized in all human societies. Therefore, it is believed that they may be natural. We can say that every part of our face communicates: a frowning forehead signifies concern, anger, or frustration, a wrinkled nose shows annoyance, and a smile means the confirmation of availability for dialogue.

Regarding eye contact with the speaker, it's about how the eye is drawn to the subject. During about 80 percent of a conversation, our eyes are walking on the partner's face. Avoiding contact is a sign of shyness or anxiety. In an official meeting, maintaining a triangle between the eyes and the center of the forehead convey the message of seriousness and interest. In a friendly meeting, the gaze is in the form of a triangle between the eyes and mouth. In all scenarios, eye contact is essential. If this contact fluctuates, the message is faulty. Proper eye contact means continuous contact for at least 30 seconds.

A person looking up is currently visualizing something in his mind. A horizontal gaze means experiencing an acoustic mental process, and looking down reveals concern for his internal state. For 90 percent of right-handed people, remembering something from the past is accompanied by eye movement to the left. Imagining future plans is accompanied by eyes that go to the right. Therefore, because this is an unconscious action when the speaker talks about how much he worked the night before to finish his tasks while his gaze slides up and to the right, you have the chance to listen to a variant of what actually happened.

Communication occurs through frequent tactile touch, such as shaking hands, hugging, and so on. Most of these gestures denote a familiarity between partners. The arms and hands are "tools" in negotiations. In the rest position, while the person is standing, they hang down freely. When sitting on a chair, arms and hands are relaxed in your lap or on the arms of the chair. Hand contact is the culmination of preparations for the opening of trading. The negotiation partner will consider you soft and easily manipulated if you provide a soft and flabby hand during a handshake.

Shake hands differently with different people. Hand contact, along with other signals, is a valuable indicator of personality. Rigid, authoritarian people will force the partner to return the hand face up. Conversely, those who reach the palm up have a defensive nature, always ready for unconditional surrender. Aggressive people, especially those who cover their uncertainty in this way, use their hands like a vise.

Avoiding involvement in the relationship is shown in rapid withdrawal from hand contact. This is what is recommended: comprise the entire palm and allow your palm to be comprised by the other's palm. The contact is firm without being rough, and hand peeling is performed simultaneously as your partner. Usually, a handshake lasts three seconds. Holding hands in pockets may mean uncertainty. Touching the hand means pointing out when someone is lying or trying to lie. Of course, this should be interpreted according to the context.

Most unconscious movements of those who lie include comforting the chin, covering the mouth, touching the nose, rubbing the cheek, caressing the hair, or pulling the ear lobe. Taking the hand to the mouth expresses the tendency to possess us. This sort of motion is often in response to something reflected on the face that must be hidden or censored, preventing anyone else from gaining information from the expression. The head resting in the palm denotes boredom; on the contrary, a hand on the cheek shows extreme interest.

When people feel frightened, they often feel the desire to have something in their mouth; the most common forms are smoking and chewing gum because they are quiet. Smokers often use cigarettes to calm and control anxiety. Posture communicates the social status primarily that individuals have or want to have. A dominant person tends to keep his head tilted up; a submissive person will keep his head down. In general, bending the body forward means interest in the partner, but sometimes it means anxiety and concern. A relaxed position, leaning back in the chair, may indicate detachment, boredom, or excessive control. It may also mean defense to those who believe they are superior to their conversation partner.

Crossing the arms over the chest means withdrawal. Crossing the arms symbolizes a certain inability to defend, so it also includes a certain degree of subordination to the partner. It also expresses the need to defend oneself. For some people, this is part of a submissive gesture or expressing reverence to someone or something.

Soldiers in the army stay with strong arms and hands along the body. It is a posture that shows submission and wisdom without reflecting simple obedience. It means obedience to the role played in the given situation and towards a superior. The person who keeps his legs stretched when sitting on the chair feels safe. Standing with legs apart denotes indifference. The more the legs are removed from each other, the greater the indifference, although it could also reflect the desire to sit comfortably, lack discipline, or lack of education.

When a person sits cross-legged between two people, you will find that the knee of the covered foot is pointing in the direction of the person perceived as more sympathetic. A hand against the hip with the elbow pulled out increases the strength and power that emanates. The proud, arrogant people show this posture in order to produce the impression of dominance. When hands and arms are kept under the table, the person is not ready to cope; he is afraid to show his hands or believes that his hands will betray his insecurity, excitement, and nervousness. If your hands are on the table, it reflects the ability and desire to establish a contact.

Personal presence. You can communicate, for example, through body shape, clothing, perfumes, jewelry, and other accessories. Tall people are often put in senior staff positions that involve direct contact with customers due to the respect that is sometimes attracted by their height. Studies show that people with pleasant appearances are considered more credible than those with less charm.

An "artifact" refers to clothing, jewelry, perfumes, cosmetics, hairpieces, and so on. They are used as an extension of the person wearing them and t0 create an image of that person. The clothing can be used to create a role in negotiating situations. Clothing and accessories can mark real or pretended social status. For example, women who attend a high managerial function will tend to dress in a sober two-piece suit and carry men's accessories, such as a briefcase.

The best impression is given by wearing clean clothing. It doesn't matter if it is a legitimate clothing item of a particular style or an imitation of it. Clothing, as the result of personal choice, reflects the personality of the individual. It is a kind of extension of the self and, in this context, communicates information about it. For example, nonconformist clothing communicates that the carrier is original, socially rebellious, or a creator or artist. Active, communicative, extroverted people choose brilliant colors, but paler colors denote introversion.

Chapter Eight

HOW TO FRAME YOUR OFFER THE RIGHT WAY

I f you're an effective negotiator, the deals that you negotiate will always be win-win solutions. This is the hallmark of a really great negotiator. There's something in it for you, and there's something in it for the other side. In fact, the best deals are win-win solutions, not just because everybody walks away with optimal results, but they're more likely to do business with each other in the future. That is the ultimate victory because when you create a win-win situation, you build trust. Of all the other people your counterpart can cut a deal with, you deliver.

You are able to give them what they're looking for while getting what you came for. They're more likely to want to seek you out than take a chance with somebody else who might not deliver the same results. While there's a possibility that they may get a better deal elsewhere, there's also a lot of risks. We'd rather go with something that we already know. Keep this in mind when trying to frame your offer. It has to be a win-win situation.

Please understand that the way you position your offer will greatly impact whether the other party will think they stand to gain or lose. That's how important it is. This is why you can't just do this on autopilot. You can't assume that you just lay out the price since you have the best price, and everything will fall into place. That's assuming too much. That's assuming that the other party will clearly see the value you bring to the table.

Please understand that people fall for bad deals all the time. You may have the best deal in town, there's no doubt about that. Otherwise, you shouldn't be surprised if the other party somehow is convinced that somebody else has a better deal.

Successful framing is crucial. It's all about laying out options for your counterpart. These have to be manageable options, and these have to be clear. They can lose if they don't take your deal, and they stand to gain tremendously if they take your deal. Seems pretty basic, right?

The Power of the contrast effect

When you present several offers at the same time, you're essentially lining up different options you're offering to the other party. This appeals to their psychological need to look at the best deal. Which of the options make them feel that they are getting away with the best possible outcome?

All of us have this built-in psychological need to come away with the best option. Knowing that this is the case, you have to arrange your options so that the other party is more likely to pick the option you want them to pick.

In a November 2011 study published in the journal Psychological Science, researchers found that when a single word in a message is changed, it drastically impacted people's behavior reading that message. The study involved healthcare professionals who were asked to wash their hands.

The researchers put up 66 dispensers which were made available to nurses and doctors in a hospital. They would then measure the amount of gel and soap used during the 2-week observational period.

They tested two signs: The first sign focused on personal consequences to the person being reminded. It read, "Hand hygiene prevents you from catching diseases." The contrasting sign focused on the effect on patients. It read, "Hand hygiene prevents patients from catching diseases." Finally, they also put a third sign, the control message, which read, "Gel in, wash out." Each of the signs was randomly assigned to each of the 66 dispensers. Please note that there was only a one-word difference between the personal consequences and the patient consequences sign. After the two-week observation period, the team weighed the amount of gel and other items left in the dispensers.

When comparing the amount of product use before and after the signs went up, the researchers concluded that hand hygiene product usage went up when the sign focused on the consequences to the patient. On the other hand, dispensers that had the sign warning about personal consequences and the control sign didn't show any change in usage.

This experiment shows that just changing one word can alter the convincing power of a message. This is all about framing. When you frame your offer, be careful with every word. They have a strong impact. They can make your offer look more attractive or easier to resist.

Use clear and manageable choices

One of the worst ways to come to an agreement is to bombard the other party with all sorts of options. If they have a long laundry list of choices to make, don't be surprised if they take a long time or they don't make any decision at all.

Obviously, people don't want to make a mistake. We are, after all, dealing with their hard-earned money.

Make the process easier for them by offering manageable choices.

Researchers wanted to test the longstanding assumption that when people have a lot more choices to choose from, they're more motivated to make a decision. They set up a series of experiments. In one experiment, they put up a jam-tasting booth in a gourmet food store. On one weekend, shoppers were invited to taste six different jam options. The next weekend, shoppers were offered 24 different jams to taste test.

All the jams on offer were available for purchase. While the larger number of jams got many more people interested in trying them out at the tasting table, these individuals tasted the same amount of jams as the previous weekend, where they only had six options to choose from.

Interestingly enough, 30% of the people who were given only six jam options to buy ended up buying a jar. However, of those who were exposed to 24 types of jams, only 3% bought. This research concludes that when given an offer, it has to be manageable to the other side. You can't overwhelm them with so many options and so much complexity, and they tend to freeze.

So while they do enjoy what you have to offer, they're less likely to make a decision. When framing your offer during negotiations, make a choice as manageable to the other side as possible. You have to do this even though people normally say, "Give me as many choices as possible. Give me your whole list." or "I want to see all that you have to offer."

They can do that, and they do, but if you follow through with that, you're not doing yourself any favor because they end up being overwhelmed. So keep it simple. Try to boil down your best deals or offers into a small manageable number. These have to have enough contrast with each other so as to make it easy so people will have an easier time choosing among them.

Multiple equivalent simultaneous

This technique involves putting together several proposals that you think are equal and valid. They are all equally important to you. You then present it to the other side. When you do this, you show your hand to the other party.

You tell them in so many ways that what issues are most important to you? The way they react, on the other hand, reveals what their priorities are. This is basically a way of reading each other in terms of priorities, and an agreement can be crafted based on which options matches which priority.

Of course, you have to do this within the framework of manageability. You can't just come up with so many different proposals that you think are equally valuable to you, but it ends up confusing the other side. You have to boil them down into a manageable number.

By offering multiple options, you're likely to increase the counterpart's satisfaction with one of the offers, leading to a higher chance that both of you will come to an agreement.

Step-by-step procedures for effective offer framing

Step #1: Frame your offer based on your goals

The first thing that you need to do is to pay attention to the outcome that you desire. This is fundamental; you have to start here. You can't just create an offer because you want to please the other side, and that's not going to work.

You have to focus on what you're getting out of it. What is the outcome that you are shooting for? And then, from there, frame your offer. It's important to step through the issues that are involved with your goals.

For example, you're obviously looking to maximize profit while at the same time, you're trying to increase the likelihood that this person or this company will do business with you again in the future. There's also the possibility that they would spread the word about your business.

So you have to balance these competing issues so you can come up with an offer that meets many different outcomes.

Step #2: Provide the best possible options

The key here is to look at your offer and see the likelihood that your counterpart will find value in the option.

You can't just say, "Well, this is the price, I'm just going to lay it out." There has to be an opportunity for common ground there.

Step #3: Present the offer in manageable terms

When you're making an offer, present it in a way that's easy to understand and doesn't have too many moving parts. The more options you bombard the other party with, the less likely you will get to yes. Why? They might see the value in what you have to offer, but you have so many things to offer that you end up confusing them.

When people face many options and are confused, they are more likely to just hesitate.

Step #4: When your counterpart puts up resistance, refrain from the issue quickly

If the other side puts up an objection, pivot and asks them, "How can we improve the situation? How can I improve this offer?" The key is to get to the root of their objection. Are they saying that it costs too much money? Are they saying that it's going to take too long, or it's too soon? What is the issue?

And see if you can concede on that while compensating on another level. For example, they say it's too expensive. You can re-frame by saying, "Okay, I can lower the per-unit price, but can you agree to a larger volume? Or can you agree to a subscription or recurring purchase?"

There are many ways to play this. The key is not to stop at No or to get distracted and sidetracked by objections. Objections can and do come, expect them. You cannot just get blindsided and end up putting up a fight or otherwise giving off signals that derail negotiations.

CONCLUSION

From the ancient concept of trading to the modern art of negotiation, the skills involved in achieving our goals will always be an area that we seek to improve, and that can have a powerful effect on our lives. Whether in business, international relations, or simply in our daily lives, we will always need to communicate and negotiate with those around us. The more successful we are at negotiating, the more likely we will achieve our goals and build good relationships with others.

Successful communication is at the heart of all types of negotiation. Without first being able to communicate effectively, we have no chance of entering into a meaningful negotiation. If the person we are trying to negotiate with cannot understand what we are trying to say, then negotiation will quickly come to a halt. Common communication barriers include a lack of self-awareness, a lack of mutual understanding; a lack of interest or relevance to one or more parties; and a lack of connection on an emotional level.

In order to overcome these barriers and engage in successful communication, we should seek to:

- Listen carefully to what others are saying
- Balance the number of questions and statements in a conversation
- Be expressive and adjust our tone, volume and body language that we are using according to the situation
- Seek to allow everyone an equal opportunity to participate in the conversation
- Accept other people's opinions and 'agree to disagree.'
- Change the topics of conversation so as not to dwell too long on negative or uncomfortable issues

Amongst the numerous aspects of what constitutes successful communication, one particular element to consider is our choice of words. We all know certain words that can be emotive, hard-hitting, or trigger a particular receiver response. Most people subconsciously choose their words for specific purposes, like using simple words to speak to a child, business jargon with your boss and slang with your best buddies. To be able to consciously harness the power of words in negotiation situations can be a powerful tool to guide the conversation in the direction you require.

Often we are looking to use persuasion to ease the process of acquiring our desired outcome from negotiation. Knowing how to phrase your words to influence the other person's response is an important aspect of the art of negotiation.

Research has shown that despite the use of words being a complex subject, simple adjustments such as the use of the words 'now' and 'because' as well as keeping a polite and respectful tone by using 'please' and 'thank you can have a significant effect on how your message is received. Being conscious of the words that we choose, and viewing them as powerful allies in the art of negotiation, can assist us in creating a positive working relationship where successful negotiation can take place.

When negotiating either bilaterally or multilaterally, we should look carefully at these working relationships and how we relate to the other parties involved. Three main aspects can be considered: the common interest that has resulted in the negotiations taking place; the divergences and consensus of each party's interests; and the willingness of those involved to cooperate and compromise to reach a mutually beneficial agreement.

It is essential to consider that negotiation is entered voluntarily and therefore can also be withdrawn from. To avoid a possible failure in negotiation, relationships between the negotiating parties should be navigated mindfully and with a strong sense of reciprocity so that the communication continues and can result in a shared agreement.

About the author

Mark Davies is an executive coach and business consultant to professional serviceorganizations and their leaders. His experience and knowledge come from more than 20 years of experience in a multinational financial company. In addition to his coaching and speaking programs, he has written and successfully published many articles, books and workbooks.

UP

URANUS
PUBLISHING

www.ingramcontent.com/pod-product-compliance
Lightning Source LLC
Chambersburg PA
CBHW071700210326
41597CB00017B/2256